Singapore
SAMURAI

Singapore
SAMURAI

Penrod V. Dean

Kangaroo Press

First published in Australia in 1998 by Kangaroo Press
an imprint of Simon & Schuster (Australia) Pty Limited
20 Barcoo Street, East Roseville NSW 2069

This edition published 2000

A Viacom Company
Sydney New York London Toronto Tokyo Singapore

© Penrod V. Dean 1998

All rights reserved. No part of this publication may be
reproduced, stored in a retrieval system, or transmitted, in
any form or by any means, electronic, mechanical,
photocopying, recording or otherwise, without the prior
permission of the publisher in writing.

National Library of Australia
Cataloguing-in-Publication data

Dean, Penrod. 1914-
Singapore Samurai
ISBN 0 73180 961 0

1. Dean, Penrod. 2. Prisoners of war - Australia. 3. World
War, 1939-1945 - Japanese. 4. Prisoners of War - Singapore
- Changi - Biography. I. Title
940.547252092

Cover design: Anna Soo

Set in Century Schoolbook 10.5/13
Printed in Australia by Macphersons Printing Pty Ltd

10 9 8 7 6 5 4 3 2 1

Contents

1. The setting sun 1
2. Prelude to battle 11
3. Beuna Vista village 20
4. Time is running out 28
5. We enter the cage 35
6. Escape from Changi 45
7. Our Chinese friends 61
8. Sabotage 90
9. Scratch two Japanese 108
10. Betrayal 119
11. Kempi Tai HQ Johore Bahru 122
12. Kempi Tai HQ Singapore 131
13. Japanese court martial 145
14. Outram Road Gaol 147
15. The second year 169
16. Return to Changi 178
17. The Japanese surrender 193
18. I join the Indian Army 197
19. Commander of a POW camp 204
20. Witnesses to war crimes 212
21. Japan 223
22. Homeward bound 240

Appendix: Tokyo War Crimes Trial 246

Dedication

This book is dedicated to Bunny my darling wife, friend and companion whose support and encouragement has nurtured me for the last sixty years. It is also dedicated to the memory of all those who went through the dark days in Outram Road, Singapore — especially my friend in escape John McGregor and R. W. (Bill) Smith, a Malaysian planter now resident in Australia, who has supported me with his friendship for over fifty years.

ONE

The setting sun

It had been a hot, humid day, although it was becoming cooler as we entered Singapore Harbour in late January 1942. Japanese bombers had just attacked the city and there was panic and devastation in the area where we landed. Even though we could have helped save those trapped under the rubble we were loaded hurriedly onto waiting trucks and whisked away.

We were quickly taken across the island to the north coast, facing Johore Bahru, and dumped on the side of the road in an area we knew later as Woodlands. We had no rations, information or ammunition, but were told to set our guns up facing Johore. It was now nearly dusk, but we could make out on our left the dim form of the Causeway that joined Singapore and Johore, and we could hear the rumble of guns only a few miles north of our position. In these trying conditions we did the best we could with what we had, although we had no idea exactly where we were, who would give us orders, or who would supply us with the many items we desperately needed. All our gear had been transhipped onto another vessel when we moved from the *Aquatania* several days out of Singapore and we had not seen it since. Tomorrow I would have to seek answers to our many questions if we were to be of any use in the rapidly approaching conflict. However, that evening the enemy were the vicious mosquitoes which were attacking us in force.

As I lay there looking over the Straits of Johore, my mind wandered back to South Perth, where I was born in 1914 and spent so many happy days growing up in preparation for what now lay ahead. I grew up in a lovely old family home with verandahs all around, facing across the Swan River to Crawley. The beach in front of our house was white and clean, the river as yet unpolluted. I spent as much time as I could in or on the water in my small dinghy with its lantern-type sail. In the summer, as dusk was nearing, I used to drift along the edge of the deep water. When the blue manna crabs came in to feed I would jump overboard in water up to my waist and scoop the crabs into the bottom of the boat. Some evenings I caught up to fifty crabs, which a local fish shop bought at twopence each — it was very good pocket money in those days. I also swam a lot and entered many long-distance races with moderate success. My other great interest was the South Perth Zoo. Its director, Ernest Le Souef, took a keen interest in my future and I spent a number of my young years accompanying him on his rounds within the zoological gardens and to his property at Serpentine, where he had nearly 100 Shetland ponies (his favourite mode of transport was his pony-drawn buggy). At well over six feet tall and with a large drooping moustache, he was one of Perth's better known figures. He was a superb veterinarian who loved all animals as much as they loved him, and most of what I learnt was acquired while I was with him.

By comparison, my father was a quiet, gentle man whose great love was eighteen-foot skiffs. He used to race the champion skiff *Yulki* on Saturday afternoons, when the Swan River was a vast panorama of yachts of all sizes, but none could match *Yulki* for speed or carry as much sail for its size. My mother was a woman before her time. She drove a monster of an eight-cylinder Fiat with gay abandon, was a skilled seamstress who made all our clothes, even my school suits, a wizard cook, and a great organiser who managed to put us all through college when finances were at a very low ebb. As if this wasn't enough, she also painted pottery — in fact I don't remember anything she was afraid to tackle. In my early years I could consider myself one of the lucky ones. At least that was the case until my father returned from a trip to England with a serious chest infection from which he never recovered. We were completely devastated when he died aged only fifty-six.

Everything had to change. My younger brother was only halfway through his education, so I had to leave school immediately and search for a job. This was in the heart of the Great Depression, when men with degrees were lining up at soup kitchens. However, I finally secured a position with Wunderlich's tile and shop fitting factory in East Perth. I had to take readings of the tile kilns during their firing, keep all the production records and assist in the planning department of the shop-fitting factory, where I drafted the plans prepared by the architect in charge. The pay was ten shillings per week. I quickly learnt to do some of the original plans and acquired all the knowledge that I could from the architect, as I was particularly keen on that type of work. The hours were long, however. I had to leave home at 7 a.m., and as I was given more and more to do, I often didn't get home until well after 9 or 10 p.m. My mother wanted me to leave as I was becoming run down, so I approached the manager for a raise and shorter working hours. He turned me down flat, believing that I wouldn't leave as jobs were so hard to come by. When I gave him a week's notice he was furious and finally offered me a raise to stay, but I knew things wouldn't work out as he and I were far from compatible.

My determination paid off and I got a job with Claude Neon, selling advertising signs. I enjoyed the work and was soon making quite good money. This was the pinnacle of my life, as I met a very beautiful young lady, Bunny Molloy, and promptly fell head over heels in love. The only problem was that the competition was keen and I had to ward off some very strong suitors. Bunny was seventeen, just five feet tall, and as slim as a reed and with an infectious Irish sense of humour. I knew I couldn't face the future without her, though she was only mildly interested in me and it took a lot of time and sweat to convince her that we were made for each other. Her father was even harder to convince, but finally we became engaged. We were both pretty young and our parents were keen for us to wait, but the world was moving quickly towards war and we seemed to realise that our time together might be limited. So later that year Bunny gave up her job and we married, moving into a small apartment near the university in Crawley. We later moved into a better and larger flat in Subiaco and as the dark clouds of war threatened, our first child, Sandra, was born.

I had spent a number of years in the militia and as the war progressed many of my friends enlisted. Knowing that sooner or later I would have to do the same, I enlisted in the RAAF as so many of my close friends had already done, but they put me on hold. After a while I decided to enlist in the army, which was taking recruits in immediately. I didn't let on that I had already applied for the air force or that I was in the militia and before long I was called up. After a thorough medical check I was sent to Northam Camp, where men were coming in from all over Western Australia. I received quick promotion to corporal and was soon called before the camp commandant to see if I was prepared to go to an Officer Training School in New South Wales. I agreed and was promptly sent on a short leave, promoted to sergeant and then sent to Sydney, along with twelve others, where we attended the Randwick Machine-Gun School.

At Randwick we were in for a shock. The school was run by members of the Australian Staff Corps. They were a tough lot who quickly told us that they would work our guts out. There was no walking and everything was done at the double. They had us on the move night and day, cramming the usual six months training into half that time, but when we left we were pretty well versed in the Vickers machine-gun. Sadly, they only passed four of the thirteen West Australians and a similar proportion from the other states.

On arrival back at the Northam Camp the four of us were interviewed by Lieutenant Colonel Ankertell, who was in the process of forming the 2/4th Machine Gun Battalion. He checked us over individually and finally offered each of us a platoon. I was given 7 Platoon in B Company, with Captain Tom Bunning in charge of the company. Most of the men allocated to the platoon were great guys, but we also had a few who for a variety of reasons would have been a liability and I had to gradually get them sent back to the training battalions.

Colonel Ankertell was determined that his battalion would be fighting fit and he marched us over long distances, setting one company against another. Anyone who couldn't take it was weeded out and after a few gruelling months the battalion was moved to Woodside Camp in South Australia. It was not a particularly happy choice as the camp already had a militia battalion in the area. They were promptly called Choccos and fights broke out just about every night at the canteen. About this time I fell foul of the adjutant of our battalion and was given almost continual duty as the town picket officer, responsible for keeping the peace, rounding up the drunks and cleaning out the brothels. We were kept busy, sometimes getting the worst of the brawls, along with tons of abuse. This was not a job likely to make you popular with the troops.

Our next move was to Adelaide River in the Northern Territory. We travelled by rail to Alice Springs and from there by truck. It was a terrible trip as the road was in the process of being reformed to carry the heavy traffic that the war was to bring to the north. Dust penetrated every part of your body and entered every bag. The food was full of grit and at the end of each day we could have joined some of the Aborigines we passed at a corroboree and never be noticed. Finally we reached the railhead below Darwin and made the rest of the trip on the oldest and roughest railway in Australia. At Adelaide River we set up camp under mango trees as high as eucalypts. The fruit, which fell continually, smelt like turpentine and I believed that I would never again eat a mango.

After a few months the Japanese bombed Pearl Harbor. When the news came through we were hastily despatched to Darwin to round up all Japanese residents and pass them onto the military police for eventual internment. They were very quiet and we had no problems with any of them.

The Japanese entry into the war caused a great flap in Darwin. Sentries were posted in all areas that were thought to need extra security, barbed wire was erected on all the beaches, and training suddenly took on a more serious tone. We knew that we would not stay at Adelaide River much longer, and there was wild speculation as to where we would finish up. When we received advice that we were to embark on a Dutch vessel in Darwin Harbour, the rumours flew thick and fast. No time was wasted in getting us loaded and we sailed out of Darwin without any advice as to where we were heading. Two days later we entered Port Moresby, where we were quickly loaded onto the *Aquatania*. Our motor vehicles and other gear was loaded onto another vessel, and that's the last we saw of the vessel or its cargo.

The *Aquatania* promptly sailed south and our next stop was Sydney, where many more troops poured on, and then on to Melbourne before we sped across the Bight and anchored just outside Fremantle. All the Western Australians on board expected we would be given at least a short leave to see our families as the battalion had been away from home for nearly a year. For some reason the smart boys in army headquarters denied us leave, but they hadn't reckoned on the determination of the 2/4th troops. They shinned down ropes or climbed through portholes and about 900 men got ashore on barges that had been loading goods onto the *Aquatania*. It would have taken another army to keep them on board. Some of the men from my platoon went to see my wife to explain what had happened, but I was not to see my wife or daughter for another four years. The best I could do was send her a telegram. The army finally recognised the stupidity of what they had done and broadcast a message to all 2/4th troops to be back at the wharf early to the next day to re-embark. Only a few men failed to arrive in time.

This time we had a cruiser for an escort when we sailed from Fremantle. Once again wild rumours flew about, but when the cruiser left us north of Australia and the *Aquatania* put on full speed north we knew we were going somewhere in Asia. The *Aquatania* was quite capable of outrunning any submarine and the whole ship vibrated as we raced through the Straits of Sunda. At Batavia (now known as Jakarta) we were again transhipped into smaller vessels. We were now within the bombing range of the Japanese, so lookouts were posted around the top deck. It was now clear that we were headed for Singapore and we all knew that the battle in Malaya was going very badly. Our forces were continually retreating south and we were particularly worried about our missing transport and equipment. Without it, we didn't represent much of a fighting force. In effect, the Japanese had already disabled the battalion without so much as firing a shot. This was only the first of many blunders that were to destroy the value of so many Australians in Singapore.

TWO

Prelude to Battle

As dawn broke and the strong, vibrant sun rose over Singapore, we saw for the first time the long thin Causeway between the island and mainland Malaya, which lay about three-quarters of a mile across the flat green waters of the Straits of Johore. Against a background of palms, the Sultan of Johore's magnificent palace stood clearly defined. A light grey mist was rising and we could see the early morning activity surrounding the area.

Even at this early hour there was a constant stream of army vehicles and personnel across the Causeway, moving in both directions to a constant background rumble of the last stages of the battle for the peninsula. However, we had other things more immediately on our mind. Each of us had spent a very uncomfortable night — uncertain of the progress of the battle and lacking even the most basic necessities. We had very little ammunition, no idea of the location of other troops and didn't even know where Company Headquarters were located. There was no water and we were covered with bites from the vicious mosquitoes. All we knew for sure was that we were on the North Coast Road. However, we took some consolation from the fact that the local population were going about their daily routine as though we didn't exist. Malays and Chinese streamed along the road, carrying baskets loaded with a variety of goods, suspended from their shoulders to some nearby market. Unfortunately no-one was carrying fruit or we would have tried to buy some.

Eventually, a runner arrived from Company Headquarters. He answered all our questions about rations and gave us some details on the current position. We were ordered to set up our guns covering the approaches to the Causeway, but with strict instructions to open fire only when ordered by the Company Commander. We were not told, however, where we would get ammunition and we had only enough for one short burst. In these trying circumstances I called the section commanders together and told them as much as I knew. We decided that we had better see what we could do to improve our situation. There was a naval base somewhere on the same road, so I sent the platoon sergeant with two others to see if they could get some ammunition and any other essentials. Another sergeant and two men were sent off to see what they could do to overcome our other major problem, which was transport. It was impossible to move Vickers machine-guns, ammunition and all our other gear without some vehicles. When the party came back from the naval base they told us the navy was prepared to make available plenty of ammunition and had most of the other items we were short of. At about the same time the second party returned driving an old Ford truck that they had taken from a small warehouse after giving the Chinese owner a receipt in General Blamey's name.

The truck, with several men and the sergeant, went off to collect ammunition and other stores from the naval base. The canteen also sold them enough breadfruit and eggs to give the platoon a light breakfast. Later that morning a vehicle arrived bringing us a reasonable amount of food and I received a long handwritten note from Captain Bunning giving me an up-to-date picture as it had been given to him. All the troops on the mainland would soon pass over the Causeway on to the island and the Causeway would then be blown up, isolating Singapore from the mainland. Naturally we were interested to see if that included the pipeline which carried the water supply to the island.

The last troops to cross the Causeway were the Gordon Highlanders, with bagpipes leading the way. Once they were all across, the demolition took place. The pipeline was still untouched, but it left a walkway for the enemy to use. Within an hour, the Japanese troops started to appear and we could soon see at least 200 of them moving about. We waited in vain for someone to decide that we could open fire as they were within range of our guns and we could have caused havoc, but it was not to be. We just sat and watched. In keeping with this blatant stupidity, nothing was done to demolish the tower on the Sultan's Palace, which was about five storeys high and allowed the Japanese a complete view of the island. In fact strict orders were issued that no-one was to fire at the tower throughout the battle for Singapore. The Japanese quickly appreciated its potential and set up an observation post to control their artillery, pinpointing all the vital areas. We were only given a few short hours before they brought up their heavy guns and started to plaster the areas near the Causeway. From then on we were never free from their very accurate fire.

A runner came to take me back to Battalion Headquarters for instructions. We made our way back through the rubber and Lalang in an area that was receiving periodical shellfire. All the platoon commanders had been assembled and Colonel Anketell advised us that, in line with the role for which we had been trained, each of the platoons would now be detached and join infantry battalions. Our own battalion would for the time being become non-existent.

I was ordered to report to Colonel Pond, Commanding Officer of 29th Battalion, which was encamped about half a mile behind our position. The 29th were in the process of trying to rebuild the battalion, which had suffered heavy losses fighting on the peninsula. Unfortunately, they had received a large number of replacements who had arrived on the same vessels as we had. Many of them had only been in the army a short time, had very little training, and had never even used a rifle. I made my way to the 29th Battalion HQ where I met the second in command, Major Fred Hore, who was nearly a nervous wreck from trying to sort out the multitude of problems he faced trying to assimilate the untrained replacements while Japanese shells fell in the area.

Major Hore had little time to worry about me and quickly said I could take over an area adjacent to two large oil tanks. I very politely said nothing doing, as the tanks would be an obvious target. Grudgingly, he allocated me another area at some distance from the tanks. Two days later the tanks were bombed from the air and went up with an almighty roar.

In view of the urgent need to get the 29th's new members into some semblance of usefulness, it was every hand to the pump as we drilled each one enough to help keep him alive when the fighting really started. For all this we were regarded by many within the 29th as a nuisance and were treated like the tail on a donkey — the last to get rations and the last to know what was going on. We had always believed that we would be welcomed with open arms as we represented a powerful defensive force with our four Vickers machine-guns and their heavy fire power. The platoon itself was restless after sitting on the waterfront watching all those Japanese troops and not being allowed to open fire. We were already fighting a crazy war while, as we heard later, senior officers were still going to Raffles Hotel for afternoon tea parties.

To make us just a bit more uncomfortable, it started to rain. With the great clouds of smoke from the burning tanks nearby, everyone soon acquired a dark oily skin. This was to stay with us throughout the battle for Singapore as the oil tanks throughout the island were bombed in turn.

We hadn't been able to find any other vehicles. The 29th Battalion had lost most of theirs on the mainland and could not help us, so we had to rely on our old Ford truck, which was an easy target for the planes which now flew unopposed above us. The artillery shelling also increased in tempo as the Japanese prepared to attack. At the same time, General Percival had made a completely wrong assessment, believing that the Japanese intended to attack in force on the north-east shore while in truth the attack was aimed at the north-west, where the troops were thinly spread with no prepared defences — the result of interference by the civilian bureaucracy who insisted that better preparation would undermine civilian morale. This stupidity cost many many hundreds of soldiers' lives and Percival must be held responsible for his weakness in dealing with the lazy, indolent department heads in the Singapore government.

Early in the morning we learnt that the Japanese had landed on the north-west coast of the island. The defenders fought heroically and killed large numbers of the Japanese, but were soon overwhelmed. Once ashore the Japanese faced no further obstacles. I was advised that we would be moving to an area adjacent to the Tengah aerodrome to form a second line of defence so the forces that had borne the brunt of the Japanese landing could fall back to regroup. We understood that the plan was to assemble sufficient forces to launch a counter-attack to push the Japanese back off the island.

There were no Allied planes above Singapore at this time, even though we heard rumours daily that a large number of Hurricanes had arrived. The truth is, we were already clutching at straws. We had hardly arrived in our new positions at the aerodrome when the whole area was subjected to a heavy bombardment from the Japanese batteries in Johore. This continued throughout the night and into the next morning. The Japanese continued to pour ashore as they overran the guns and men on the coastline. Our machine-guns were now in action, firing over the heads of our own troops while the remnants of the defenders on the coast fell back through our area.

Conference after conference was called by the Battalion Commander, preparing for an advance against the Japanese troops, but at the last minute it was called off as we fought to hold the aerodrome. At about nine that night we came under fire from two sides. I sent a runner to seek assistance from Company Headquarters, only to find that we were on our own. The Battalion had forgotten to tell us when they moved out and we had to get away quickly before we were surrounded. We had no idea where the 29th Battalion had moved, so we gathered up all we could carry and struggled through a rubber plantation and then small swampy areas, seeking any signs that would help us find our Battalion. We were not to see any of them again until we became prisoners of war in Changi.

Eventually we broke out onto the Kranji Road and found ourselves in the middle of a conglomeration of troops in confused retreat. No-one had any information and most of them had lost contact with their own groups. In the middle of all this I met Colonel Pond, the CO of the 29th, who had also lost contact with his troops. He told me to join up with a mixed brigade who were trying to make a stand and gather up the troops who were out of contact with their own battalions. The Japanese had by now landed their artillery and mortars and the whole area was under heavy fire. Our weapons were of little value in this area so I decided to fall back down the Kranji Road to seek rations, ammunition and transport, and to then search once again for the 29th Battalion. Having sent the platoon into a rest area, I took Sergeant Pearson and Corporal Halligan with me and we set off down the road.

At Transport Park there were a number of Bren gun carriers which would be ideal for our purpose, but the young English lieutenant in charge of the park wouldn't have a bar of parting with four carriers unless we could produce an authority from Area Command. With our patience at breaking point, we told him we were going to take them whether he liked it or not. Fortunately both Pearson and Halligan had driven tractors, so we went back to the platoon, picked up two other men who had also used tractors, and ferried them back to pick up the other two Bren gun carriers. At last we were mobile. We still had to get more ammunition, but some of our good scroungers came back with enough to keep us going.

With everyone rested, it was time to get back into the battle and we decided to move down Buena Vista Road, which led to the west coast.

THREE

Buena Vista village

Buena Vista was one of the most beautiful villages on Singapore Island. Under normal circumstances it would have been alive with the noise of the Chinese and the Malays in their colourful clothes, laughing and chatting as they made their way about their daily business.

There were many kampongs (villages) in this area, set back in the coconut groves or rubber estates, mostly with about 100 or 200 inhabitants who have lived a happy life following their customs and old ways of living, as had generations before them. Buena Vista was somewhat larger, with many shops, a large school and a few public buildings. Buena Vista means 'good view' and it was a charming place, but four days after the Japanese had landed this was an inappropriate description. The area had been ravaged by shell and mortar fire as well as being heavily bombed by Japanese planes. The road was still taking mortar blasts as we drove down towards the village and many of the sights that unfolded before us were indescribable. The side of the road was littered with a variety of goods that the locals had attempted to take with them as they fled. Much of it could have been from looters, who by this stage were everywhere. However, whichever way they had arrived there, the owners or illegitimate owners had suffered terribly. It was a scene of carnage.

There were bodies everywhere. Some were clothed, some unclothed ... some without heads ... some without arms or legs ... some almost split asunder ... Heads lay alongside the road, their eyes staring. The putrid smell, maggots and the clouds of blowflies were as much as most of us could take. There were pieces of bodies in the trees ... and there were several pregnant women who had not lived long enough to give birth to the life within them. One image that was indelibly stamped in my mind was that of a young woman who had been almost split in half by a shell fragment, with her unborn child partially exposed as she lay tangled in a welter of blood and gore.

Some people wandered around aimlessly, even though death was creeping closer every minute, while others just sat and cried. The sounds of battle could be clearly heard through the rubber trees, but there was little we could do to ease the pain and torment as the survivors would not listen to us. Perhaps they didn't understand what we were trying to tell them. We knew we couldn't stay on this road, exposed to the planes overhead which were spotting for their artillery. So we sped through this area of unbelievable carnage with its putrid smell and on to the outskirts of Buena Vista village, where we put our carriers under cover with the intention of giving covering fire to help people escape down the Coast Road. The village was on fire and a pall of smoke hung over the area, adding a further layer of dirt to our filthy clothes. The terrified local population were running about hither and thither not knowing what to do to avoid the rain of death from the Japanese planes and the artillery, which had opened up again. The spotter plane had probably reported our arrival at the village.

There was spasmodic machine-gun fire from the north and we opened up return fire at long range, hoping the native population would listen to us and leave the area. But the language problem combined with their state of mind, made it difficult to reach them. Most of them had wounded, maimed or dead relatives in the area and for that reason, or to protect their few worldly possessions, they wouldn't leave.

We fought a hopeless battle against increasing pressure through the remainder of that day. Late in the afternoon, the carrier we had placed up the Buena Vista Road to protect our right flank came racing back. It had taken a direct hit from a Japanese tank which had suddenly appeared on the road. Sergeant David Holme and the machine-gunner were both badly wounded. We were no match for a tank, so I gave the order for Holme and the other wounded man to be taken back down the Coast Road towards Singapore and to find a hospital. The other carriers were to follow me to see if we could contact a line of defence. The Coast Road was by now a seething mass of people heading back to the city. There were Indian, Australian and English troops, all totally disorganised and without leaders. Trucks were being left on the side of the crowded road and there was complete panic. Japanese planes came over, strafing the road and causing a great number of casualties. We tried to get the Australian troops to join us but they wouldn't listen. They had had enough and many of them had already discarded their guns and equipment.

After we had travelled a short distance in this seething mass, we met an English officer from the 1st Malayan Volunteer Regiment who was trying to get some of the fleeing soldiers to join with his forces to hold a line that they had on the ridge nearby. They desperately needed machine-gun support to protect the approaches to their position. We were happy to join them and drove our carriers under the rubber, where we camouflaged them with branches. Before nightfall we were firmly in position. The Regiment was commanded by English officers whose cheerful, determined approach to their task was like a welcome breeze. Colonel Andre, the Commanding Officer, was a tall well-built man with the largest handlebar moustache I have ever seen. He was dressed in a motley collection of clothing, which included a pair of rubber Wellington boots, had a machine-gun slung over his shoulder and was determined to stay put.

Our position was the first suitable one we had occupied for our guns to do their job. We had a clear field of fire for three-quarters of a mile, covering the Buena Vista village and its approaches. Through my field glasses I could see the whole area clearly. There were villagers fleeing before the enemy and we believed that the Japanese would by now be infiltrating the mobs dressed as Chinese peasants — they had adopted the tactic of sending women and children of the village ahead to stop rifle and machine-gun fire. At a hasty conference with Colonel Andre a desperate decision was taken. I felt terribly sorry for the Colonel, because he obviously had to struggle with his conscience before he made it. If we were to hold our position, then infiltration by the Japanese dressed as Chinese must be stopped, otherwise they would cause havoc and force a withdrawal. So it was agreed that we must open fire on the road junction when prearranged signal flares were fired from Battalion Headquarters. Knowing that we must slaughter innocent people as well as the Japanese soldiers, I called my section commanders together and told them of Colonel Andre's difficult decision. The sun was down and night had started to fall, so we would not be able to see the result of our firing. But we dreaded the dawn.

By 9 p.m. we were receiving heavy mortar fire searching out our positions. The Japanese had occupied the village area in force and were trying to locate the strongpoints holding up their advance. The Malay troops dug in above the Buena Vista Road had observed Japanese assembling in the rubber in preparation for a move against their positions and the signal flares were fired from Battalion Headquarters for us to commence firing. Our guns were in action most of the night, chattering their hymn of death as we laid down heavy barrages of fire on all areas adjacent to the road junction and the village. Few would escape this merciless fire as we poured thousands of rounds over the heads of the Malay troops. Even above the sounds of falling shells and mortar we could hear the cries and screams of the wounded and dying.

The Malayan troops took heavy casualties through the night as the Japanese launched attack after attack, but they sent out constant fighting patrols to clean up any Japanese trying to infiltrate their front line. As the fighting continued, we were desperate for water and food and sent a number of men to scrounge whatever they could from nearby houses. Any supply operation had long ago broken down and we had to constantly seek ammunition wherever we could. Much time was wasted in filling empty belts of ammunition for the guns. Our foragers came back with a variety of food taken from houses and shops further down the Coast Road and a few kerosene tins of water. There was barely enough water for both drinking and for the cooling systems of the guns and we had no hope of washing off the filthy film of oil that covered us and our equipment throughout the fighting. We were a dirty, stinking mob of Australians, but buoyed by the happy, determined fighting unit we were now attached to.

By dawn it was already hot and steamy. The day was going to be another terrible one and we could count on the Japanese throwing new troops into the area. As the sun rose we could see the carnage that our guns had created during the night. Buena Vista village had virtually been destroyed, the road was covered with craters and bodies lay everywhere. I could see through my glasses that many of them wore Japanese uniforms, but there were also many civilians. I had no idea how many of them were Japanese dressed in Chinese clothes and could not ponder it long as, under a barrage of shells and mortars, the Japanese launched a fresh attack against the Malayan troops. The Japanese were sitting ducks as they advanced and they fell in dozens as our four guns concentrated fire on them. The distance was ideal for us to achieve a thick spread of bullets as they came out of the rubber. It was as though they had run into a wall and I doubt if a rabbit would have made it to the road. A mortar shell fell near one of our guns but the crew miraculously escaped with minor injuries. However, the Malays were taking heavy losses from the accurate and blistering mortar bombs pouring on their positions.

Suddenly the Japanese withdrew, the firing stopped and there was almost a silence. But the fighting intensified on our right flank where the troops were again forced to fall back. A runner called on me to report to Colonel Andre, who told his company commanders that he had been ordered to fall back to a new position in line with the troops on his right flank. He said he had no intention of moving at this stage, as the position was strongly held, but that he would advise us quickly to withdraw if the situation changed. We were then given the map reference of the fall-back position. Throughout the morning the Japanese launched probing attacks to try to find a weak spot to attack, but whenever they showed themselves we dropped a wall of fire on them. During the night the Japanese had brought up two tanks to attack our position, but the Malays were prepared and launched successful attacks on them with Molotov cocktails (bottles of petrol with wicks) — neither the tanks nor their crews escaped.

Desperate to force the Malayan Regiment to retreat, the Japanese set fire to the scrub. As the wind drove flames and smoke towards our lines, Colonel Andre gave the order to fall back to the arranged map reference. Unfortunately, the new position would not give us the same scope to use our guns to their full potential.

FOUR

Time is running out

On 9 February we were positioned across the Pasar Panjang Road, only a few miles from the centre of the city of Singapore. In a few short days we had been pushed back about eight miles and at this rate we had little time before we would be fighting in the city itself. And judging by the flood of humanity that was jostling down the road, there seemed little hope that the tide could be turned in our favour.

There were trucks, armoured cars, motorcycles, wheelbarrows, oxen and carts. In fact, anything that would carry people or goods was trying to move on the road. And there were thousands of soldiers — Indians, English and Australians — all fleeing, pushing and jostling to try and reach Keppel harbour, with only one thought ... escape. Colonel Andre and some of his officers tried to get the soldiers to stop and fight, but they all refused to listen or take any notice of his orders. No-one could stop this flood of humanity as they made a bee-line for the harbour. The Japanese, however, were in no hurry. They knew that the thousands flooding into the city area would force a breakdown in all administration and make their attack easier, so they waited until the road became less congested, though their planes strafed the roads and bombed the throng of vehicles and people. A group of twenty-five bombers dropped their bombload down the road towards the harbour, with appalling results.

These wonderful Malays we had been fighting with must have had very mixed thoughts when they saw what a rabble the Indian, English and Australian troops had become as they fought and shoved. However, they made no comments and concentrated on digging shallow defences against the attack they knew was inevitable. I will never forget the quiet, confident way in which they cheerfully carried out whatever task given them, ignoring the chaos that surrounded our area as we set about preparing for the next attack. Meanwhile, the Japanese had adopted the tactics they used so successfully on the mainland, continually moving fresh troops into the battle against troops who were tired, without rations, fed up with the lack of information, bereft of leadership and fully aware that there was no hope of any relief. It is little wonder that so many gave up and tried to escape.

That afternoon I sent a party back into the city to try to get supplies, water and ammunition. When they returned with some of these items they reported chaos. The harbour area was a mass of people fighting with each other in their attempt to force their way onto the few remaining ships that were loading wounded and hospital personnel. Even the smallest boats were being commandeered by dozens of men, determined to escape no matter what, who used their rifles to gain possession. While all this was going on there were snipers in some of the buildings, picking off people at will. No-one seemed to take much notice of those killed or wounded. The locals knew full well that the Japanese were going to occupy Singapore and those whose sympathy lay with them now came out into the open and set about settling old scores.

The returning party also reported that mass looting was going on and that they had great difficulty in finding food, though they had been able to secure a lot of ammunition from abandoned trucks. In the lull we attempted to bury a number of our dead. Wherever possible we took their tags off, but many did not have any identification. Before we could complete this gruesome work we were advised that the Japanese were preparing to attack again. They did this under a heavy cover of fire, led by officers brandishing their swords, but they received a hot welcome. The first wave was wiped out very quickly but they continued to come through the rubber, wave after wave, finally giving up and leaving behind hundreds of wounded and dying. After dusk they tried sending smaller groups to find a way through. Some of them did penetrate our lines but they didn't last long. The Malays were far better at fighting in the dark than the Japanese. Eventually, however, the troops on our right were forced to fall back and Colonel Andre decided to withdraw a further half mile to maintain our contact with them.

The decision was a wise one as the road was now an impassable mass of burning vehicles. It took us a long time to cover the short distance as we had to carry our equipment and weave our way through the unbelievable mass of discarded equipment, dead bodies, and goods of every description. Anything we had to leave behind we destroyed, which was I suppose a pretty futile gesture when you consider the mass of army equipment that had been left on the sides of the road by the fleeing troops.

Now that 100 000 or so fighting troops were concentrated in a much smaller area we were receiving more information. But we all felt the net tightening, and the water position was critical. The island's reservoirs were in the enemy's control and they shut off the supply, which had been only a trickle anyway, with so many pipes broken and pressure almost non-existent. What little we had we strictly rationed. At one stage, when we were close to a brewery, I sent a couple of men to see what they could scrounge, but they came back empty-handed. All they could find were quantities of malt and hops.

February 10 and 11 were days of hard and critical fighting as we fell back short distances, trying to maintain some cohesion with other units still fighting. The Japanese knew that victory was close and threw everything they had against to force the issue. Their 18th and 5th Divisions had been constantly attacking us since they landed and their Guards Division had tied up large numbers of our forces on the north-east coast where General Percival wrongly believed the main attack would take place. Once the Causeway had been repaired, the Guards Division streamed onto Singapore Island with their tanks and armoured vehicles and quickly drove across the island, forcing General Percival's troops into retreat.

On 12 February we received orders from 8th Division Headquarters to leave the Malayan Regiment and report back to an area where all the Australian troops were being assembled into a perimeter within which, the story was, we would fight to the last man. No-one told us where the water, ammunition or rations were to come from. However, it was an order and we prepared to move out. We were all very sad to leave Colonel Andre and his magnificent Malays, who had provided us with the only stable fighting force we were to know on the island.

We made our way back along Robinsons Road, past the mass of people still hoping for a miracle in the harbour area. It was difficult to find the location we were seeking as none of us had been in the area before, but when we finally reached the assembly point we met up again with other members of the battalion for the first time since we had landed in Singapore.

Everyone was tired and dispirited and rumours spread quickly. My Company Commander, Tom Bunning, had not yet received any instructions so we had to wait or further orders. No-one was too pleased with the idea that we would stay put and fight to the last man, but some of our concerns were even more immediate. Not only were water and ammunition in short supply, but our location was an unsafe one. We had no shelter or trenches against the mortar fire the enemy was now bringing down on us and it was impossible to dig in. However, we did the best we could with what we had, and settled down to await developments. We spent a very uncomfortable twenty-four hours being constantly shelled, with the usual spotter plane circling overhead. On the morning of 15 February we were told that we had surrendered and were now prisoners of war. All our weapons and other equipment were to be piled up while we waited for further instructions from the Japanese.

It had taken the Japanese just eight days to force the surrender of the supposedly impregnable fortress of Singapore. They took it with a much smaller number of soldiers, who overwhelmed the defenders largely as a consequence of the inability of our generals to meet the threat with proper coastal defences, or organised reserve forces to push the Japanese back off the island once it was established where their main attack was taking place. The defending forces were not cowards but they fell apart because they had neither support nor leadership from competent commanders. Consequently, they were never able to re-establish a cohesive defensive strategy or position. Each day the confusion became worse.

Supply had broken down, the inability to maintain communications contributed to the systematic destruction of opposition by the Japanese, and the hordes of people falling back into the city area made reorganisation nigh on impossible. Books published after the war record that the Japanese couldn't understand how they were able to use the Sultan of Johore's place tower as an observation post throughout the battle. They were equally surprised by the ease with which they were able to take control of the reservoirs and the water supply, and by the masses of equipment left without any attempt at destruction. The Japanese were able to supply their troops from the food dumps captured and were astounded by the continual retreat of the opposing forces.

They had taken the island with enough supplies for a year and the bulk of the equipment, including the floating dock, in serviceable condition. The population were subdued and the biggest problem was what to do with more than 90 000 captured soldiers.

FIVE

We enter the cage

After the turmoil and noise of battle, an unnatural hush descended and we were able to take stock of our position. We were a motley, unshaven, dirty mob of uneasy, tired men. Thirsty and mostly without food for the last few days, we had piled our arms and ammunition as directed and we sat talking quietly. None of us knew what would happen next.

Small numbers were foraging in nearby houses and shops, seeking anything edible or useful to a POW. Some of the inhabitants of nearby houses were now coming out into the open. Japanese flags were starting to appear on buildings and the population set about resuming their life. We were left in no doubt what the locals felt. The Malays jeered us and the Indians spat at us. The local Chinese were similarly treated — their problems were about to begin.

Most of us just lay down quietly, wondering what the future held in store. Some tried to remove the stubble of beard and most of us tried to remove some of the oily slime that had been with us since day one, but without water and soap most of it stayed firmly attached. It was not long before the rumours started to flow once again, if they had ever stopped. Some said they had been told where we were going. They were not within a bull's roar of the truth but the speculation helped pass the time as we watched the far hill, on which there was a Chinese cemetery, expecting soon to see the approaching Japanese. Eventually small groups started to appear and make their way towards us, entering and examining all the houses as they approached. They ignored Indians and Malays but the Chinese were attacked immediately. These troops were the sons of Nippon who had fought the Chinese in Manchuria and China, where great cruelty had been handed out by both sides.

Purposefully, the Japanese troops pillaged their way through the nearby compounds, savagely attacking the Chinese and their womenfolk, who fled from the houses but were soon caught and dragged back inside. The Chinese in Singapore could expect no mercy from their new masters.

The first patrol that reached our area comprised about a dozen Japanese, led by a stocky sergeant with a heavy black stubble. For most of us, this was the first time we had seen Japanese soldiers close enough to assess their build. They were all pretty small and bandy-legged, dressed in sloppy grey-green uniforms, bandoliers, peaked caps with a red star on them, puttees and black canvas split-toed boots. With fixed bayonets, their rifles were almost as tall as they were.

They approached us warily, speaking harshly

amongst themselves. Seeking to ensure that no-one had any arms, they looked over the piles of rifles before they came closer. With their rifles pointed at us, they were an unfriendly looking bunch. There were two trucks nearby into which we had loaded all other surplus gear, in the hope that we could take it with us wherever we were going. The soldiers examined the trucks carefully and then by signs indicated that they wanted men to drive them. No-one wanted to be in it and we were all scared stiff. Past experience on the mainland had shown that anyone taken to drive a vehicle was never seen again. Finally they grew impatient and herded two men into the vehicles, indicating that they would kill them there and then if they didn't obey. None of us was able to speak Japanese and it was impossible to interfere. Eventually they all piled into the trucks and took off towards the city. The two men taken to drive did not turn up again.

Later that day we received information that we would be marching to an area known as Changi the next morning, where we would start our POW internment.

Next day we set off on the thirteen-mile march to Changi, on the north-east tip of the island. It was in a beautiful area known as Selerang, where the British Army troops were stationed before the war. Facing across the Straits of Johore, Selerang had housed 2000 soldiers prewar, but now it was going to house closer to 90 000. As our ragged column moved along the Coast Road we could see what had happened to other parts of the island during the battle. The road was pockmarked with shell holes, most of the houses and shops were damaged and many of them had been completely gutted. The occupants who had survived were now ferreting in the ruins to see what they could salvage. The Malays and Indians turn out to jeer at us as we marched past but the Chinese, who represented the bulk of the population, were conspicuous by their absence. Practically every house or building sported a white flag with an oval red centre. This was immediately nicknamed the 'Fried Egg' and this name was to remain through the rest of our POW days.

The march to Changi will be forever remembered by all who took part. We had little water and it was a dreadfully difficult march for those who had minor injuries or wounds. The Japanese had refused to provide more than three vehicles to take those who were incapable of walking, so these had to be used to shuttle the sick and those who had to quit the march. A hospital had been set up in Selerang and was quickly filled with wounded POWs and those who fell out of the march from sheer exhaustion. With a limited number of halts for a rest, we stumbled along without food and with little water, each of us with his own thoughts. Sometimes a Chinese family took the risk and brought water and food out to the passing troops, but our captors beat them if they saw any of them anywhere near us. In the afternoon we passed the Changi Gaol, where the Japanese were to hold the civilian internees, and where troops were later to replace them.

In prewar days the Selerang Barracks had been a magnificent area with three-storey concrete buildings for the garrison set around a large parade ground. There were, in addition, football fields, tennis courts, and the officers' quarters — two-storey houses set in beautiful gardens and coconut palms. Before the war this must have been one of the most desirable of postings.

However, we were tired and dispirited and our chief concern was how the barracks were going to accommodate such a vast number of troops. Some rudimentary planning had been carried out by Headquarters and about 110 men were to occupy a house that was designed to take about six. The house to which we were allocated was bare of fittings. Everything had been stolen except for a bath and a wood stove. We were starting from scratch, as though we had been washed up on a desert island, and were thrown on our own resources. We were hungry, but everyone was so bushed that our primary concern was to find a spot to lie down and rest. Somehow we all managed to doss down, but it was very difficult to sleep. No-one was used to the crush of bodies or the smell, and the area was alive with mosquitoes. Some of us talked quietly, others snored or spoke in their sleep, but very few were able to get more than an hour or two of unsettled sleep. We all knew that we would have to organise some better way to allocate the room available.

The next few days were spent trying to organise some equitable distribution of the few resources we had carried into the camp, as no rations were yet available from the Japanese. Parties were sent to collect coconuts, others to break them open and others to search for tins or utensils. Other parties were sent out to search for firewood, to dig trenches for latrines, to cart drinking water or to collect sea water to evaporate for the salt content. During those first days everything edible in the area disappeared. It was as though a plague of locusts had descended on Singapore Island. Ripe and unripe coconuts were the first to be attacked, and the immediate result was an outbreak of diarrhoea and dysentery amongst all those foolish enough to eat them. Every day men were dying in the hospital, as there was an acute shortage of drugs even at this early stage of our captivity. Bandages were also at a premium and operations were carried out in fairly primitive conditions.

The camp commander negotiated with the Japanese every day for a supply of rations, drugs and other essentials, even down to spades, but always the reply was to be patient — that we would have what we needed later. We soon realised that this was to be the standard Japanese reply to any request and that it didn't mean that they had any intention of doing anything. On the third day the Japanese trucked a quantity of rice and a few vegetables to the camp, along with a limited number of tins of bully beef, a small quantity of medical supplies, some kerosene tins and a few large kwalies to cook the rice in. However, none of us had any idea how to prepare rice in vast quantities and the most unpopular troops in the area were the cooks who turned out a sloppy, half-cooked dish of rice which had been boiled in salt water. We were issued daily with one tin of meat, about sixteen ounces for forty men. The rice was about one pint per meal, issued three times a day. The rice issue stayed at about this level but the meat soon ran out.

The Japanese told us that we would have to grow our own vegetables and that they would issue what they could in the meantime.

Those early months sowed the seeds of destruction of many thousands of POWs who later died in work parties all over Asia. You could see men losing weight, colour and vitality every week. The unusual diet, the lack of fruit and vegetables, the long and monotonous days and the depression that came with being a POW all combined to wreck their health. There were, however, those who refused to just sit and wait. The will to survive outstripped all other things and they searched more diligently for anything edible. Snails, lizards, even rats were consumed.

Gradually, organisation took over and conditions for everyone improved, even though the rations were never sufficient, didn't get better and were never adequately complemented by the vegetable gardens. Additional work parties gave most of the men something to occupy their thoughts, and classes were set up to teach an amazing variety of subjects.

I had already decided that POW life was not for me and was determined to escape while the Japanese were still reorganising the civilian population. The war, I believed, would last a long time and I would have more chance of survival if I got away from Changi, even if it meant only breaking away to get into the jungle and fend for myself. I believed that I could at least find sufficient food to survive on the Malayan Peninsular. However, I did not fancy doing this on my own and realised I would need a compatible person to go with me. I quietly broached the idea of escape with a number of reliable guys that I could travel with, but most of them were not prepared to take the risks involved, and many were scared stiff of the idea of living in the jungle for any length of time.

However, a short, thick-set corporal in the Company Headquarters, John 'Mac' McGregor, had also made his mind up to escape at the first opportunity. Mac was a quiet, determined man, and even though he was a full twelve years older than me, I knew he would be a well suited and reliable companion. We spent several days discussing every aspect of what we would face, raising various ideas and scenarios and arguing the pros and cons of each one.

We agreed that it was useless to consider going south to Australia. The distance and difficulties were just too great to overcome, and as the enemy was continually moving south it would be almost impossible to get through. We knew Sumatra had been occupied and that the battle raged in Java. On the other hand, the case against escaping the jungle took into account our lack of local knowledge and the hostility of much of the local population.

The Japanese commander in Changi had already announced that escape was impossible and that the penalty for any attempt was beheading. Not only that, but a substantial reward was available for anyone helping in the capture of escapees.

Mac and I concluded that our best chance lay in making our way across the Straits of Johore to the Malayan mainland and into the thinly populated east coast area. By travelling north, avoiding all towns and Malays or Indians and seeking to make contact with friendly Chinese, we could then make our way across to the west coast where we would seek to secure a suitable sailing boat — preferably a junk. We would then travel up the coast at night, hiding up during the day, until we were far enough north to make a dash for Ceylon (Sri Lanka). The Japanese had the area covered but we believed that their main commitments were down south and that a small boat may escape their attention long enough to get us free.

McGregor and I did not discuss our plans with more than a few trusted friends. There was already some suspicion that the Japanese were getting information from somewhere in the camp and it would be all too easy for someone to give us away in return for a reward and better conditions from the Japanese. We also had another problem closer to home, as our own Battalion Commander, Major Green, had issued a directive that anyone attempting to escape would be handed over to the Japanese for punishment. Mac and I were particularly upset by this direct contravention of the established order. At any rate, we had to be doubly wary of any possible leak of our intentions.

By way of preparation, we decided that we should make a number of reconnaissance trips by night, out of the camp and down to the coastline facing Johore. Our aim was to check out local habitation, see if we could secure a boat to get us across the straits, and seek any other information that would be useful. There were many obstacles we knew we would face, even in the early stages of our escape, as the tide rose and fell considerably in the area, the currents were quite fierce, there were many fish traps nearby, and a shipping boom. It was essential that we take a good look at the area beforehand and try to line up a boat to use on the crossing.

SIX

Escape from Changi

The next few days were very busy for me and for Mac. Careful not to arouse any suspicion, we spent as much time as possible hunting down information from various people who had knowledge of the area — especially some of the English soldiers who had been stationed at Selerang Barracks before the war. We did not feel bound by Major Green's orders not to escape as we understood it to be all captured soldiers' objective to escape or make the enemy use as many troops as possible guarding them. POWs in Europe were very active and had forced the Germans to put more troops into inactive areas to stop prisoners from their continual attempts to escape. Certainly, it was more difficult to create similar problems for the Japanese.

Some of the English soldiers were a fund of information and what they told us helped us draw up a plan and devise a method of crossing the Straits of Johore. This preliminary planning was simple compared to the task of accumulating enough food to see us through until we were well away from the coast. We reckoned that we should avoid any contacts for at least a week once we were in Malaya, and that the further inland we could get before we had to seek food the safer we would be. It was also imperative that our contacts be limited to the Chinese, as most of the Indians and the Malays wouldn't hesitate to turn you in to the enemy for the reward, which was more than they would normally earn in a year. At this early stage of the occupation, both the Indians and Malays had a lot of respect for the ease with which the Japanese had disposed of the Allied forces.

Our ration problem was solved for us with the assistance of the Company Sergeant Major and a few other supporters, who put aside some of their daily rations to help us build up a supply.

The next move was to make a preliminary inspection of the area between the camp and coast, including the native kampong where we hoped to get a boat. I crawled through the wire late on the night of 12 March and made my way down to the kampong. All the villagers were asleep and it was a very spooky experience, but I found what we were looking for. Under a jetty there were a number of boats, including a prau which would be ideal to take us across the Straits. As well, there were a lot of large concrete pipes nearby, along with a few sheds and European-type houses which would provide us with plenty of cover. I had to be careful getting back into the camp, as Indian guards were supposed to regularly patrol the dannet-wire perimeter fence. Fortunately they were a lazy lot who patrolled the area irregularly, so I crawled back inside without a hitch. I was back in camp and asleep by 2 a.m. Only those few in the know were aware of what I had been up to.

Mac and I decided that we should confide in our Company Commander, Tom Bunning, as we did not believe he would let on what we were about to do. He was not enthusiastic when he heard of our plans, but he raised no objections and guaranteed to give us at least a week before he reported our absence to Battalion Headquarters and the Australian Camp Commander.

Mac and I believed that we must take off as soon as possible to ensure that only we were at risk. We had already strained our luck and the more time passed the likelier it was that someone would accidentally reveal our intentions. So Mac and I bade our farewells to all those who had helped make our attempt possible and gave them bits and pieces of equipment we would not need on our journey. It was an emotional time as we did not know whether we would see any of them again.

Quietly, at about eleven that night, with our meagre food supplies, a map that we had made up from others in the camp, and a compass but very little else, we made our way cautiously to an area in the fence where I had already cut the wire the night before. We waited until the Indian patrol was out of sight, then crawled through the prepared opening and swiftly made our way towards the village.

As we approached the jetty close to the now slumbering fishing village we heard a motor vehicle approach and promptly we dived into one of the nearby concrete pipes. Our hearts were pounding as a Japanese patrol pulled up and debussed six soldiers, who made their way out to the end of the jetty. They stayed there for hours and we were trapped until the early hours of the morning, when the soldiers eventually climbed back in their truck and drove away.

This delay meant that there was no way we could escape that night, as we didn't have time to paddle across the Straits before daylight. And as we could not risk being seen in the open, there was no alternative to finding some secure place to hide through day and to make our attempt the next night. Around the outskirts of the jetty there were a number of houses and buildings that must have been used by the British army before the war. Many had been hit by enemy shells and we reckoned they offered us our best chance to get cover for the day ahead. We stumbled around in the buildings for some time and eventually discovered a cellar where we could pull some timber over the entrance and wait for the night.

We slept fitfully in this dank space for the next few hours, until we were woken by the sounds of activity as the nearby village awoke. Both Mac and I were sore and itchy from the attention of hordes of mosquitoes that had feasted on us. As the day progressed, the noise from the kampong increased. Dogs barked, children played noisily and we had a number of narrow escapes from detection as parties of Malays who had been detailed to clean up the area wandered through the buildings. Occasionally they walked directly overhead, but fortunately they seemed to be more concerned with a nearby building which must have offered better building materials.

It was very difficult to maintain absolute silence in such a small area for so long. We were so cramped up we couldn't stretch our legs, and it was almost impossible to make a meal. In fact, all we could do was eat some cold cooked rice and take a drink from our water bottles. As the evening approached and the villagers returned home we cautiously climbed out of our hide and made our way down the jetty. The boats that had been tied up there when I had made my first visit were gone. Our only hope now lay in taking one of the boats that the villagers pulled up on the beach not far from their houses. Wherever possible, they liked to stow their canoes under their houses so we were going to have a difficult time securing one without making enough noise to set the dogs off.

We crept quietly towards the outskirts of the kampong searching for a suitable prau. When we crawled in between houses we could hear the natives talking. Some of the dogs growled at us, but fortunately they didn't attract their owners' attention. Eventually, towards the far end of the village we found a small prau with a paddle in it. Someone must have been intending to go out again, probably to visit one of the large fish traps spread through the Straits. We quietly picked up the prau, carried it to the edge of the water, loaded in our gear and climbed aboard. It was a very small craft and by the time we and our gear were on board there was little freeboard, so we would have to be particularly careful not to overturn.

As we pushed off on the next stage of our adventure, it was very dark. The moon had not risen and we could only vaguely make out the end of Ubin Island, about half-way across the Straits. Using this as our guide, we took turns at paddling our way towards Malaya and freedom. Our biggest worry was the phosphorescent water which threw an eerie glow on both sides of the prau. We made slow progress and had to stop a number of times as native fishermen with lamps aglow approached us. Each time we swung around behind them, making our way towards Malaya a slow and winding one.

We had been paddling for about an hour when we reached the submarine boom that protected the naval base. It was made of large drums supporting a heavy steel net. There was no way for us to cross this net, so we had to paddle along it to try and find an opening. When we eventually found one we scuttled through without incident, but just after we got clear of this area a searchlight was turned on from Ubin Island which brilliantly illuminated the whole area at the opening of the boom. Native craft were supposed to observe a curfew after dark. However, many Malays ignored this edict and carried out their usual night fishing. At this stage the Malays were happy with the Japanese and were not yet afraid of them. We passed under a number of fishing traps next to which were shacks built on poles that stood just above high tide level. Some of them had families living there and we were particularly careful as we continued on our way. It took us another three hours to reach the Malayan side of the Straits, but we could be thankful that we had achieved it without being seen. The cloudy night had helped us, but the clouds were clearing and we were glad when the Malayan shore loomed up and we paddled into the entrance of a creek. The whole area was mangroves and smelly mudbanks.

Most of southern Johore and the east coast is fringed with mangroves and swamps. We selected this area to land in as it was also sparsely inhabited and we hoped to get inland without having to dodge around too many villages. As soon as we found a suitable place to get ashore we unloaded our gear, left the paddle in the prau and pushed it back into the Straits, hoping it would float a long way away before it was found. With a bit of luck it might even be carried back to the far side by the tide and it would be assumed that the owner had just been careless.

We had little hope of moving far in the remainder of the night, so we tied our haversacks to a mangrove, crawled up into a most uncomfortable spot and settle down to wait for the dawn. This was how we spent our second night of freedom. We didn't manage any real sleep as the mosquitoes were giants and when one of us dozed off we would almost fall out of the tree.

The hours to dawn passed slowly. When we finally crawled out of the tree and onto the muddy ground below we were full of aches and pains and ravenously hungry. But we had no chance of cooking any food here so we gathered up our gear and set off, using our compass, to try and find solid ground where we could make a meal. The heat increased rapidly as the sun came up and we knew we were in for a hot and steamy day. It took a long time to travel only a few hundred yards and we were soon filthy from the mud, covered in scratches and feeling very low. However, the land gradually rose and, leaving the mangroves and mud behind us, we moved into the edge of the jungle. Here again our progress was very slow as we had to cut our way through thick undergrowth, but finally we came into a small clearing where we flopped down exhausted. After a short rest we gathered up some leaves and dry timber, got a fire going and prepared a decent meal of rice and some dried fish. After finishing our first hot meal since leaving Changi, Mac and I spent time cleaning as much of the mud off our legs as we could, though there seemed little point in being too fussy until we reached a creek.

However, we now had another problem as the area was alive with leeches which quickly worked their way up under our pants and down our socks. We were continually forced to stop and take our boots and socks off to get rid of them. What with the leeches and the clouds of mosquitoes, we were in real trouble — we had to push on and get away from the swamp into a rubber plantation as soon as we could. At one stage Mac remarked that he would rather face the Japs than stay here with the mozzies.

So we gathered our gear and set a compass course due north, pushing our way through the heavy undergrowth. Occasionally we had to deviate around obstacles, but we always returned to our escape route, hoping to put as much distance as possible between us and our landing spot. Needless to say, we had no idea whether our escape had been kept secret from our Headquarters or from the Japanese, and we couldn't know if the Malay whose prau we had taken had reported it missing. But we knew we must act as though the worst had happened and play for safety and distance. At one stage we came across a large swampy area and had to wade through it, sometimes up to our waist in stinking brown water. The swamp was alive with leeches and our tempers had become pretty frayed by the time we emerged to find ourselves on the edge of a road and not too far from a kampong.

There were lots of Malays and Indians moving around and we had no choice but to cross the road to get into the rubber plantation on the other side as quickly and unobtrusively as possible. It was imperative that we move before someone spotted us and we badly needed to get rid of the large number of leeches feasting on us. There was not much traffic but we would be in clear view of the kampong. A further complication was a number of attap houses nearby. We had no idea if they were inhabited and hurriedly discussed what we should do. Mac and I agreed that we would slip across the road one at a time, when we thought the coast was clear. I went first, when a truck had pulled up in the kampong and everyone's attention was taken. Mac followed a few minutes later and we quickly moved into the safety of the rubber trees. It was a good thing we moved when we did, as a truck full of Japanese soldiers pulled into the village not long afterwards. There was probably a military post in the village, but come what may we had first to strip off our boots and get rid of the leeches. They weren't hard to get rid of and in fact dropped off on their own accord, they were so bloated with our blood.

Gathering our gear again, we took off into the rubber, continuing north. Late in the afternoon we reached a wonderful, beautiful babbling creek of crystal clear water gurgling over the rocks like gentle music. We were safe here, deep in the rubber and away from any habitation, so off came all our dirty gear to be washed thoroughly and hung out to dry on the low shrubs. Then Mac and I set to with relish to get rid of the grime and filth of the swamps. Still in our birthday suits, we cooked some rice and made a billy of tea. For a while we felt like kings. Free, and masters of our own destiny, we were tired and quietly settled down to a peaceful night during which we gave no thought to the dangers that lay ahead.

We were up and about at first light. After a quick, simple breakfast, we boiled water for our water bottles and, with shaven faces and clean clothes, we set off again on our trek north. About three hours later the rubber finished and we hit the edge of another stretch of jungle. This time it was much more dense and proved very difficult going, but we eventually broke through at the edge of another patch of muddy swamp. Not knowing how long it might take us to get through, we stopped to rest and eat the remainder of the breakfast rice, washed down with a good strong cup of tea. The swamp was only about two feet deep, but lousy again with leeches, decaying foliage and roots that slowed down our progress. After several hours we heard voices and sounds of another kampong. We quietly made our way to the edge of the swamp where the scrub began.

Once again we had reached a narrow road used to service the villages in the area. In the distance to our left was a small bridge leading to a village. There were a number of peasants on bicycles and now and again a small truck passed by. We kept well hidden in the scrub and quietly discussed our next move. It seemed dangerous to go west, so we pushed on to the east, away from the village, and looked for a quiet place to cross the road. To do this we had to re-enter the swamp but we hadn't travelled far before we were suddenly faced with a vast stretch of water which looked both deep and dangerous.

Given the choice of crossing the road and facing more swamp or waiting until dusk and creeping over the bridge and through the village, we decided to take the second option and spent an uncomfortable time waiting for the villagers to go into their homes for the night. Mac was swearing quietly to himself as leeches were attaching themselves to him as fast as he removed others. The mosquitoes were also very thick on the edge of the swamp, so we were losing blood faster than we could hope to make it.

Gradually the light faded, the Malays retired to their houses and the village became quiet. While common sense dictated that we should wait for it to be much darker, we opted to make our move while there was still enough light for us to see where we were going. We were so miserable from the mud, leeches and mozzies that we thought the risk was worth taking. The ground rose higher on the far side and would take us further away from the swamp. We tried to move quietly but our boots seemed to make a hell of a row as we crossed the bridge and moved past the houses and small shuttered shops. Unknown to us, the Japanese had a post here. Our first knowledge of its existence came when we saw through a window several Japanese soldiers eating a meal, talking loudly and singing as they drank their saki. We had other narrow escapes when some of the natives moved across our path, but we froze until they were inside again. Our rations were now at a low ebb and we had eyes for anything we could filch that would supplement our larder. In Malaya it was normal for each family to have a chicken house, usually a cage above ground level, in which a few straggly chooks were cooped up at night.

On the outer edge of the village Mac moved off towards one of the chicken houses. It was a pretty big risk he was taking, as the chook would kick up a row once he grabbed it unless he was very quick, so I moved over to a position where I could keep an eye on the house. An even bigger risk was that there might be a dog nearby, but I don't think Mac would have let a dog interfere with him that night. At any rate, Mac was very quick and quiet and by the time he joined me again he had nearly plucked the chicken. Not thinking, he continued to pluck it as we moved on into a rubber plantation, leaving a trail of feathers. We stumbled on for some hours, with only a few rest stops, before we stopped at about midnight to prepare our evening meal, get rid of the usual lot of leeches and clean off the dirt acquired during the day.

Before we could cook the chicken we needed some way to hide the fire in case we were close enough to civilisation to be seen. We searched around until I literally fell into an ideal place. It looked like a slit trench and must have been dug when the battle passed through this region. We soon had a fire going and the scraggy chook was put in our billy to boil. What a meal it was — chook, rice, some vegies and a strong cup of tea.

We were beginning to believe we were going to make it and, having taken off our sweaty clothes, we sat naked in the bottom of the slit trench, free even from the constant attack of the mozzies, which were driven off by the smoke from our fire.

The chook was pretty tough, but it was a gourmet meal to us and all we left were the bones. I sat at one end of the trench and Mac the other, smoking one of our strictly rationed cigarettes, laughing and talking over the trials and tribulations of the last forty-eight hours, but I suppose we were both apprehensive of what lay ahead. Both of us knew it was going to be extremely difficult to find our way from one side of Johore to the other. Our map was pretty rudimentary and showed only a few of the features we needed to negotiate if we were to cover the distance and find enough to live on. We discussed these problems and agreed that our best bet was to approach Chinese farmhouses for assistance. Many of the Malays and Tamils had sided with the Japanese, but the Chinese knew what the Japs had done in their homeland.

Next morning I awoke with a start to the sound of voices nearby. We were both so tired we had overslept and sunlight was filtering down through the rubber trees, where the tappers were already at work. As I peered over the edge of the slit trench I jiggled my foot against Mac to wake him. Several hundred metres away some Tamil women tappers were collecting latex from the cups which were attached to each rubber tree, beneath slits in the trunk. Fortunately they were working a fair distance from us, but for one horrified moment I imagined the Tamil women coming along to find two Australians, naked as the day they were born, sleeping in the bottom of the slit trench.

By this time Mac was awake and had his head up to the edge of the trench. We dressed ourselves as quickly and quietly as we could and gathered our gear, ready to move away from danger. Mac was worried that there may be many more tappers nearby. This must have been one of the plantations the Japanese were trying to get back into production quickly as they were desperately in need of rubber for their war machine. As far as we could see in all directions there was nothing but rubber trees, so there was nowhere to hide or lie up for the day. Our only chance of escape was to keep going north, keeping a sharp lookout to see that we skirted any compounds or workers.

Despite our chicken meal the night before, we were already as hungry as horses, but we could do nothing to prepare a meal, not that we had much food left anyway. Things looked pretty grim and our friends the mozzies also reminded us that we must take our quinine tablets if we were to avoid a bout of malaria. They we lousy to take at any time, but with our supplies of water strictly rationed, the taste stayed with us for hours.

After travelling north for a few hours without seeing anyone else, we struck the edge of the rubber and sighted a house in a fairly isolated position right on the edge of the jungle. Mac kept watch as I approached the farmhouse, which was typical of those built by Chinese farmers, with an attap roof, a pond at the back, a small pig pen and a chook house. I had no intention of going to the house until I was sure that it was occupied by Chinese. Before long a Chinaman came out and headed for the outhouse, which was built over the pond.

I waited until the farmer started to return to the house before I called out to him. He stopped, gave me a startled look, and started to run to the house. Then he suddenly stopped and called out to me in Chinese. I had no idea what he said but I picked up the 'Japon' and I realised he thought I must be Japanese. 'Australian!' I called back. He still didn't seem to understand and I could see he was very frightened. However, when he eventually realised I was not Japanese his fear seemed to evaporate. He started to talk quickly to me, but I indicated I didn't understand, so we fell back on signs to show what we were after. Fortunately, hunger signs are universal and when I finished my performance he pointed towards the house. So I waved to Mac to come on in and we followed the Chinese farmer into his home.

SEVEN

Our Chinese friends

The house comprised only two rooms, one to live in and the other to sleep in. It was a simple arrangement. All cooking and washing took place in the living area, where grain and farm implements were also stored. There was a table, some stools, a small fireplace made from firebricks, the usual kwali, an old hurricane lamp and an odd collection of dishes. A greasy looking curtain covered the entrance to the sleeping area.

It is always very difficult to tell the age of the Chinese, but I would think the man was in his late fifties, while his wife was probably in her middle twenties. They had two young children. The wife and the children were shy, and probably very much afraid, but the farmer had us sitting at the table and quickly produced several chipped and greasy bowls which his wife filled with food. The meal was a mixture of vegetables and some sort of meat we could not identify. But it was hot and we were hungry, and very grateful that these poor people had without any hesitation fed us what was most likely their own meal.

Mac was particularly fond of children and encouraged the farmer's two small children to come a little closer as he spoke quietly to them in broken Malay. Finally he had them on each knee, and as their trust grew the farmer went out and brought in what were obviously some of his most precious possessions — a bowl of black eggs. Mac looked at me with horror. As hungry as we were, neither of us was keen to tackle the Chinese eggs which we knew had been buried for a long time, but we owed it to this gentle man to put on a brave face and each take one. When we peeled the shells off, the insides were hard and evil smelling, and I still don't know how we managed to get the eggs down.

While we were struggling with the ancient eggs, the farmer told his wife to make up a parcel of food for us. We knew they could ill afford this, as they were already living at a near starvation level, but they were generous to a fault. Finally the wife brought us two parcels of cooked rice and some cooked tapioca root. We tried to explain to her how grateful we were, then made our goodbyes as the farmer led us to a path at the edge of the jungle. From his gestures we understood that the path would take us through the jungle but we must have seemed uncertain and our guide finally took Mac's hand and led him part way along the path to make sure we understood what he had been telling us. When we both started to move forward, he returned to his family, who we could still see standing outside their house.

After several hours we reached the far side of the jungle and another large rubber plantation.

In the distance, smoke rose from another kampong. It had started to drizzle, there was thunder in the air and we had to find shelter in a hurry if we were to avoid a very miserable time. Keeping well away from the kampong, we made our way towards an isolated building that looked like a small schoolhouse, which is what it turned out to be. We checked it out, found that it was unoccupied, pushed open a window and climbed in. Within minutes, the rain came down in sheets and continued throughout the night, accompanied by violent claps of thunder. There were a number of mats which the children must have sat on, so we were able to make ourselves comfortable, eat a meal and spend the most restful night since our escape.

When we awoke in the morning, the sun was up and it was already a hot, steamy day. As it was still quite early we decided to light a fire and heat up some of the rice and tapioca for breakfast. We had just finished our meal and started to pack our gear away when we heard the approach of a motor vehicle. Mac was already packed so he took off through the window, but I was still finishing my packing as a truck pulled in and stopped in front of the building. I was out the window in a flash but unable to run into the rubber without being seen so I crawled under the building, which was a few feet above ground, just as Japanese soldiers piled out of the truck and opened the door to examine the building. As they stamped about over my head, chattering away, I lay there quietly. I could see their legs as they moved between the vehicle and the building. Two or three of them stood out the front and in typical Japanese fashion piddled where they were. Eventually those in the building stamped out and got into the truck.

As they did this I edged my way to the back of the building, ready to make a break for the cover of the trees and join Mac. For some unknown reason one of the last of the soldiers bent down to look under the building. He got a terrific shock when he saw me and called out loudly to the others. I don't think he was sure what I was, but he soon realised that I was up to no good and the other soldiers started to pile out of the truck. However, I was well into the rubber by that time and Mac and I were running deeper into the plantation. For some reason the Japanese only fired a few shots and made no attempt to follow us. Perhaps they thought we were part of a larger group and didn't want to risk walking into an ambush.

After we had put sufficient distance between us and the schoolhouse we finally had to sit down and rest. We were both completely bushed but Mac and I had a good laugh and reckoned that when we got home again we would enter the Stawell Gift (a professional foot race held at Stawell, Victoria). There was a down side, however, as we had been forced to drop a few items on the way. Our precious kwali and some of our rations were lost, so we were almost back to scratch again. The loss of the kwali was a major blow as it was our main cooking utensil and would be very hard to replace. Our best chance lay in finding some Chinese village with a store where we could buy another one.

However, by now we had learnt the varied uses of the tapioca root, which grew anywhere where there were farmers, so we wouldn't starve. Tapioca grows underground tubers like sweet potatoes and can be ground down into a type of flour. It can be pretty stringy but is very nutritious. Even the Malays, who were a pretty lazy lot, grew small plots behind their houses. It requires very little attention and grows from a cutting stuck into the ground, so no skill is needed to produce a crop.

After we were fully rested we set off north again. Towards sundown we sighted a large European-type home which appeared to be unoccupied. We checked it out from all sides before we got too close, but we were finally satisfied that it was unoccupied. Whoever lived here had left in a great hurry. Most of the furniture was intact, as was the crockery, and there was clothing in the bedrooms.

Mac and I were like a couple of kids let loose in a lolly shop. There were four bedrooms with about eight beds, linen and mosquito nets, so we had a choice where we would sleep that night. We ransacked every cupboard and found a few odd things that had been overlooked when the owners fled, such as a jar of marmalade, a bottle of hot sauce and some very stale bread. There was even a gramophone and some records, but tempted as we were we didn't dare play them as we had no idea how far the music would carry, or how far we were from other people. Just after dusk we heard the approach of a train. It sounded as if it was about half a mile away and it took some time to get out of earshot. From the sketchy detail on our map we reckoned that we must be somewhere near Sedenak — a small whistle stop on the main line between Johore Bahru and Kuala Lumpur. This meant we were on our planned course and we decided that when we set out again we would move slightly to the east, to keep away from some of the small towns nearby.

Exploring the house further, we found the bathroom equipped with both hot and cold taps, so we traced the water line to boiler. It didn't take us long to get a fire going in it and later, after a good meal, we shaved, had a steaming hot bath and then crawled into beds that had so recently been occupied by a planter and his family. If they ever returned they would probably never know what a godsend it had been to two weary escapees. This was not a night to be repeated for many years.

Thoroughly rested, we were up and about at dawn, anxious to be on our way. It would be very dangerous for us to be close to Sedenak during daylight. We were relaxed and refreshed, and keen to move further north before we attempted to cross the main road and railway line, both of which presented real dangers.

Our legs and arms were troubling us from numerous scratches and cuts, many of which had turned septic. However without antiseptic or bandages there was little we could do other than keep the cuts clean. After we had travelled several miles north and slightly east, we sighted a village in a small valley ahead of us. There were about twenty or thirty houses and as we moved closer we observed them carefully, hoping it was a Chinese village and that there were no Tamils or Malays in the vicinity.

We knew all along that we would have to depend on the continuing, help of the Chinese if we were to escape. And that also meant we'd have to find a way of making contact with their underground forces. The village was quite isolated and appeared to be inhabited only by Chinese, so Mac and I decided to risk approaching it directly. With luck we could not only buy some food and replace our kwali, but also put out some feelers about contact with the Chinese guerilla forces. We also hoped to buy some medication and bandages for our cuts and scratches, which were a constant problem with the pus oozing from them.

It was very much in our favour that we were cleaner than we had been for days. This should give us our best chance to win the locals' confidence and help, so with an air of bravado we made our way down to the village and headed for its centre, where there were several stalls and shops. As we passed by, the Chinese took little notice of us, which immediately boosted our confidence. When we entered the largest shop we were greeted in English by the Chinese shopkeeper, who asked what he could do for us, just as if we were in a normal shopping area in normal times. We had some Malayan dollars and had no difficulty in buying a good supply of food at a very reasonable price, along with a second-hand kwali.

After our transactions were complete the shopkeeper asked us into the house behind his shop for a cup of tea. After discussing a number of other subjects we asked him about the possibility of making contact with the underground forces. He was very cagey, which was only to be expected, but when we were able to finally convince him that we had escaped from Singapore and showed him our paybooks, he became more relaxed. We also assured him of our honesty and that we would not in any way jeopardise his position.

There were a number of guerilla camps in the region, our friend then told us but they were hidden deep within the jungle and only the guerillas knew how to get to them. They were understandably cautious and distrusted everyone, even the villagers who supplied them with food, as there had been instances of Chinese spies helping the Japanese with information. No-one from the village had ever been allowed into the camps but there were some pick-up points on the edge of the jungle for food and supplies. The shopkeeper said he could take us to a spot just on the edge of the jungle where the guerillas could contact us if they wished to.

Our friend was keen for us to stay hidden in his house until dusk. He didn't think there were any spies in the village but was not prepared to take any further risks, so we settled down to rest while he went about his normal business. That evening he led us out behind his house, down to the edge of the jungle and through a well–disguised entrance to a small attap hut about a 100 yards inside the jungle. Then he quickly said goodbye and went off back to his village. We made ourselves comfortable in the hut and awaited events.

We didn't have long to wait. Suddenly, and very silently, three well dressed Chinese soldiers appeared in front of us. They were wearing jungle–green uniforms, with Japanese boots and puttees and peaked caps with a red star on the front. Each man had several grenades tied to his belt and a bandolier of cartridges slung across his shoulders. Their rifles, were not ones we had seen before, but there was no doubt that the long bayonets on them were lethal.

The soldiers stood and looked at us for a few minutes. Then two of them stood guard while the third put his rifle down well out of our reach and gestured for us to stand up and turn around. Once he had checked us over to see we didn't have any concealed weapons, he indicated for us to sit down again. Up to this point, not one of them had spoken a word. Mac and I tried a few broken

Malay words on them but they did not respond. We tried again in English, and while I am sure they understood us perfectly it seemed that they were not going to have anything to do with us. Finally two of them sat down, still with their weapons pointed in our direction, and the third soldier vanished without comment.

By this time Mac and I were wondering what we were getting ourselves into. These soldiers certainly weren't friendly and they were guarding us as though we were enemies, watching our every move. Finally, at about eleven o'clock, the guards jumped to their feet as a young Chinese officer wearing glasses and with a pistol on his belt, appeared. He sent the guards out of the hut, sat down and started to interrogate us. During the next hour or so he questioned us carefully on a wide range of subjects trying to find holes in our story. At the same time we tried to get some information from him, but he was very evasive we gleaned nothing. It was a totally one-sided conversation and his refusal to answer even the simplest question caused us both deep concern. However, after showing us that he had an extensive knowledge of Singapore, Changi and Malaya, and appeared to have contacts within the POW camp itself, the officer apologised for the questioning but said he had to be absolutely certain that we were genuine escapees. He and his fellow guerillas had already dealt with several traitors. As a dyed in the wool communist, our interrogator made no secret of his distrust of the

British but felt that, for the time being, any help they could get to attack the Japanese would be welcome. He then told us the camp was a long way off, over a very rough and twisting track, and that it would be wise to stay here for the night and set out early next morning.

Now that we were on better terms with this young officer, we found he was a very interesting man. He told us that his name was Soon and that his parents were merchants in Kuala Lumpur. Soon was a founding member of the Communist Party in Malaya, which was rapidly organising guerilla forces all over the country. His short-term objective was the defeat of the Japanese, followed eventually by the establishment of a communist Malaya. To start they would harass the Japanese lines of communications and then, when they were strong enough, they would launch full-scale attacks. Mac and I had no idea that they had made so much progress at this early stage, nor had we realised that they were so determined to take the country over when the Japanese were defeated. Reflecting on what we heard at this time and what we saw take place over the next few weeks, it is easy to understand how difficult the British found it to peacefully control Malaysia after the war.

As soon as dawn broke, the guerillas shared their rations of pork, rice and vegetables with us and we set off. Every few 100 yards Soon gave a password to a sentry we never sighted. Occasionally I thought I saw some movement, but

I was never completely sure where the sentries were. They were well concealed — no-one would be able to use this track without being observed. After some time Soon told us we would have to be blindfolded for the next section of our journey. If we were captured by the Japanese we would be unable to lead them into the camp, even if they tortured us. This seemed a reasonable precaution and for the rest of the journey we remained blindfolded, led along by the hand. This made the journey very slow as we constantly stumbled over roots and stones. We only realised we were approaching the camp when we heard sounds of activity.

Our blindfolds were taken off and after a short rest to give our eyes time to adjust to the light, we set off once more. As the noise grew louder we were stunned to see that a large calico sign had been erected at the entrance of the camp. Painted in red letters were the words, 'Welcome to our Brave Australian Allies'. We made our way into the camp through a guard of honour of about fifty soldiers. Finally the camp commandant, who we understood was a colonel in the Chinese Communist Army, greeted us warmly in flawless English. He then addressed the camp, again in English, though we were sure not many understood. He told them how Malaya would become a land of milk and honey once, with the help of the British and other allies, the Japanese were defeated. The Chinese Communist Army would be victorious and drive the Japanese out of all Asia, which would become a communist continent. He then invited us to share a cup of tea with him.

Mac and I were goggled eyed at the camp. It consisted of about thirty well-built huts, including a hospital, all made of the usual attap. They were laid out in a square, beneath camouflage netting, which was regularly replaced with freshly cut foliage. There appeared to be several hundred people in the camp including a number of young women in uniform whose armbands signified their position — usually medical orderlies or volunteers — in this well organised force. On the edge of the camp sat an Australian 25-pounder artillery piece. How they got it in there I have no idea. There were also two Bofors guns and, on the far side, a large ammunition dump on which they had a constant guard.

We went with the colonel and several of his officers into his headquarters where we were given a cup of tea and some biscuits. Mac and I were asked a continuous stream of questions about conditions in Singapore, how we escaped, what route we had used, how much contact we had had with people along the way, whether they were likely to know where we were heading and, finally, what our army training was and what we had planned to do. We explained to them that we intended to go further north and then cut across to the west coast, where we hoped to secure a vessel and escape to Ceylon. The colonel told us we would need a lot of assistance from well to do

Chinese in the area to do this. The Japanese were in strength along the west coast and had the Straits of Malacca well covered with patrol boats. However, our chances would improve if we could break out into the Indian Ocean. The Japanese were not yet well organised further off the coast, owing to their commitments nearer Java, Borneo and the islands surrounding New Guinea. There were a number of Chinese junks of sufficient size to attempt the crossing to Ceylon, the colonel told us, and if we stayed in the camp long enough he would make contact with sympathetic Chinese. It might be possible to organise an escape with the help of Chinese fishermen.

In the meantime the colonel suggested we could help them, as they had a number of Vickers machine-guns and Bren guns which they had scrounged during the Malayan campaign. In fact they had collected whatever was available from either side. He also warned us that under no circumstances could they permit us to leave the camp, as we could easily get lost in the jungle and become a liability to his forces.

We were assigned a small hut of our own, somewhat isolated from the others, and given an interpreter who was to show us around the camp. While this was taking place we met a number of junior officers, who were a pretty tough looking lot. We also learned that the colonel in charge of this camp was Liew Kim Bok, on whose head the British were to put a very large price after the war, during the Malayan 'Emergency'. He was finally killed in an ambush near Bukit Jerampang.

The following morning the camp was astir early and a comprehensive clean-up took place. Our interpreter told us that the number-one commander was to make a quick visit and we should be ready to meet him when we were called.

It had been a hot and humid night and we had found it almost impossible to sleep, though the mozzies had been kept at bay by the mosquito nets that we were lucky enough to have. However nothing could compensate for the early morning noises of about a hundred Chinese hawking and spitting, which seemed to be acceptable to the rural Chinese in Malaya, and we were revolted by the primitive washing conditions and the filthy toilets. Most of the troops in this camp were of peasant stock and seemed to have no knowledge of hygiene. The toilets consisted of an attap screen behind which they dug a number of holes and a line of people, both men and women, waited their turn to use the one, dirty facility. The smell and the constant spitting were our prelude to breakfast, which was very basic. Two cooks boiled a large tub of soup with chunks of pork and some pineapple floating around in it. Everyone sat around on their haunches and helped themselves, taking a separate bowl of rice from another tub.

Once breakfast was over the guerillas assembled on the parade ground where, accompanied with loud singing, a red flag with a hammer and sickle was raised. After a long fiery speech by the colonel, the troops broke up and went to various locations for training sessions. Later in the morning there was more shouting and all the troops lined up at the entrance to await the arrival of the guerilla commander. He was a young well-groomed Chinese wearing a well cut uniform of jungle green. After he made his way through the guard of honour, he went straight to the headquarters hut.

After about an hour a messenger arrived to tell me that I was wanted at headquarters. Mac made to go also, but was told that he was not needed. I made my way to the hut, where the commander greeted me warmly and invited me to sit and take tea. At this stage I had no idea of his name or that of many of the other officers, who always avoided my requests for their names. I later learnt that the commander was Chin Peng, who was to be the prime troublemaker for the British after the war. He was a friendly man, well educated and with a wide ranging knowledge of many subjects. We discussed the future prospects of the war and he told me that his organisation was already causing the Japanese problems. As time progressed, he hoped to engage them in much larger numbers all over the Malayan Peninsula. He refused to be drawn when I asked him what would happen after the war. When I asked him whether we could count on his help to reach Ceylon he said yes, but added that the assistance we were offered would be up to individual unit commanders. We parted on the best of terms, and he left the camp several hours later. I was not to see him again.

Mac was cheered by the information as we both had misgivings about our hosts' intentions. We sensed that the guerillas were not going to let us get out of this camp easily. From our conversations we felt that all they wanted from us was information on how to use the arms and equipment they had acquired. After further whispered conversation we decided to test our suspicions by going to the edge of the jungle to see how the guards reacted. We didn't get very far before one of the guards came up to us and indicated that we should return to the centre of the camp.

We spent the next few hours in discussion and considered the most sensible course of action. Escape was clearly impossible. We had little idea of our location and the pathways leading in and out of the camp were heavily guarded. So we decided to string along with the guerillas until something broke in our favour, but not to be in any hurry to teach them how to use their weapons. After another horrible evening meal we sat for a while beside a group of soldiers who were belting out some communist songs, then went off to bed for another restless night. We hadn't got used to the bamboo slat beds, but at least we were safe from the Japanese.

The usual coughing and spitting greeted us again in the morning, followed by another vile breakfast and a terrible wait to use the filthy toilets alongside a young Chinese girl. We felt ready for anything the world could throw at us. How these Chinese could possibly have any normal sexual interests once they had shared this part of their life I will never know. In fact both sexes were prepared to pull down their pants and piddle anywhere in the camp. I made sure that I was never too close to male or female.

After the morning flag-raising, the troops broke off into groups to start their morning training. Mac and I wandered around watching the activity and checking over the motley collection of arms that had been gathered up from the battlefields. They had a quantity of Japanese arms and ammunition, a number of Vickers guns, some Brens and even a few old Lewis guns. The ammunition dump contained a great collection of different sized artillery, shells and a quantity of mortar bombs for which they had no guns.

One of the guards told us that the colonel wanted us to join him in his headquarters, so off we went. The colonel offered us a cup of tea and biscuits, which we were happy accept after the junk we were living on. More importantly, he was most anxious to get our reactions to his camp. We were careful to tell him what he wanted to hear. Then he asked whether we were prepared to start training his men how to use the machine guns. We told him we were and he provided us with an interpreter, two machine guns, several belts of ammunition and about a dozen soldiers. We set about trying to turn a group of pretty dumb peasants into machine-gunners. The first job was to pull the guns apart, clean and oil them all, removing the rust that had developed since they were last used. Then we slowly taught the Chinese what each part was, where it fitted and its purpose.

The soldiers were attentive, though not very bright. The combination of our go-slow policy and their fairly dull intellect meant the job could be strung out to take a long time. Only a short time ago these troops had been farmers in kampongs with small holdings. The officers had come from the educated classes but these ordinary farmers, who would be the gun fodder in the battles to come, had been well indoctrinated with communist principles and the discipline in the camp was very strict. There seemed to be little control over the movement of the women, who were given a lot of tedious jobs such as uniform making and boot repairs but at no time did I see any familiarity between the sexes. All the soldiers wore dark green uniforms, puttees and either boots or Japanese slit toe canvas shoes which they had probably taken from the dead. Most carried a large knife or bayonet in their belt, and all the officers were equipped with pistols.

Living in the jungle meant that there was limited light. The sun only filtered down through the jungle canopy and the ground and the undergrowth were always damp. As the day wore on it became like a steam bath and our clothing was always wet and smelly.

About noon, we broke off for lunch, which was the usual soup with some green veggies and rice. The constant pork diet made both of us squeamish and each day we ate less soup and more rice. Eating soon became a chore, rather than something to enjoy.

One day after lunch all the officers were withdrawn to an area on their own where some heated discussions took place. We knew something was brewing but had no idea what. The colonel was shouting and appeared very angry. Finally the junior officers returned to their groups and selected a number of men from each, who assembled near the headquarters. The colonel then came out and addressed them. Our interpreter friend told us that they were going to attack the Japanese post at Sedenak later that night, blow up some of the railway line and damage the points in the junction area.

Later that afternoon we approached the colonel and asked if we could take part in the attack. He was furious that we knew about it but said there was no way we could take part. He didn't want the Japanese to have any idea that we were in the region, as they would immediately bring in more troops. The colonel left us in no doubt that he thought we were a pain in the arse and should be grateful that we had a secure place to stay. We could be very useful training the men, he added, but they would do all the fighting. About seven o'clock that night about thirty men assembled and the colonel led them out of the camp.

For most of the day we had tried to get the interpreter to give us some idea of our position and the distance to the west coast. He was clearly afraid to give us any further information, as the colonel had bawled him out earlier for telling us about the raid that night. Both Mac and I began to feel that we had even less freedom here than we had enjoyed as POWs back in Changi. So we had to plan how to get away from the guerillas. If we couldn't get permission to leave, then we would have to escape.

Next day, all our planning had to be shelved when a party of three Englishmen and two Australians were brought into the camp. They had been wandering around in the jungle since the Malayan campaign, getting food from the Chinese, and were eventually handed over to the guerillas. They were all in very bad shape. Two of them had malaria, others had suppurating jungle ulcers and they were all starving. None of them knew of what had transpired since early in the year — they had been trying to make their way south, not even knowing that Singapore had surrendered. They were stunned by our information and had to completely reconsider their plans. They certainly weren't at all happy with the prospect of staying in the jungle, especially under the control of these Chinese communists. So they planned to go north into Burma and then head for India. None of them had ever been in the north and they didn't realise the enormous difficulties they would face with the jungle and the hostile local population. Apart from those considerations, the vast distances involved meant they would need to be in first-class physical condition. One look at them was enough to show there was no way they could get into shape for such an enterprise. Mac and I had already decided that we would not accompany them, wherever they wanted to go, as they would be a drag and lower any chances of success.

Mac and I had to shelve our plans to break out, as it was imperative that we all left together. Otherwise the Chinese would take punitive action against those who remained. Our first priority was to try to get them all into the best physical condition that the food supply and conditions would allow, as we would have to put a good distance between us and the camp before anyone knew we had left. So we continued training the Chinese in the use of the Vickers whilst the others spent time trying to get their ulcers on the mend. We were able to give them quinine for their malaria so they gradually started to improve.

During the next couple of weeks the Chinese were very active. Parties left camp every day, on foraging trips, to attack small Japanese posts or to ambush convoys on the roads seeking food supplies and ammunition. Several night-time forays blew up sections of the railway tracks. They had quite a few casualties on the night ventures and the small hospital rapidly filled up with wounded, some of whom died.

When the other allied party — Titch Anderson,

Curly Brookes, Frank Canole, Jock McLaren and Bluey Kelly — seemed to be well on the way to better health, Mac and I began to think again about how we were going to disengage ourselves from this camp. We found it very difficult to come to any concrete arrangements with the other escapees. Some of them were inclined to stay put and sit out the war, which they believed would soon be over. Mac and I spent a lot of time talking to each of them on their own, to make them realise that guerillas wouldn't feed them without getting something in return. If the going got tough none of them would last long, and they should give careful thought to moving while they were in the best condition. We left them in no doubt that we had only stayed so they could recover their health, and that if needs be we would leave without them and they would have to take their chances with the Chinese.

The Chinese made their minds up for them the next day when they tied up two of their own troops for some infringement of the camp rules. They executed them and, with much laughing and joking, tossed their bodies in graves that had already been dug. It frightened hell out of us all, and brought home just how tenuous our position actually was.

Finally all were agreed that we must all leave the camp together, and then go our own separate ways. I had cooked up a good story that would allow the colonel to help us on our way and said I would ask him to give us a guide to lead us to the edge of the jungle. The colonel heard me out. He was interested in my suggestion that we could take information out to the Allies and persuade them to drop arms and a good transmitter into a friendly village at the edge of the jungle. We could be blindfolded whilst being led out of the camp, I said.

The colonel was keen to convince me that we were all safe in his camp and that his first consideration was for our safety. He was also keen to convince me that by training his troops we were also making a contribution to the war effort, but he still disagreed with me that it would be practical to allow us to go on any of their attacks on the Japanese. I think it was the possibility of his getting more arms and a transmitter that finally made him give serious thought to my request that we leave the jungle camp. We were all also aware that the supply of food was dwindling. The Japanese had tightened the noose around the local farmers, not only to stop them supplying the guerillas but also because they wanted more supplies for their own troops. The rations had dwindled week by week and we were told that a number of villages had been burnt down and the inhabitants executed when it was suspected they were supplying the guerillas with rice. It seemed logical that the Japanese would soon start to relocate all the farmers away from the edge of the jungle.

I finally made an agreement with the Colonel that he provide us with a guide and some rations to help us on our way. He would also provide me with a letter to a Chinese merchant on the west coast who could assist, us in the procurement of a boat. The merchant could be found at Pontian Ketchil in Johore, about forty miles from the camp as the crow flies, although we would cover a much greater distance to reach the village. We would be blindfolded for the trip out of the jungle.

When I returned to the others, we discussed what we would do once we were free again. The five recent arrivals had decided that they would go north as planned earlier. Mac and I said we would go west, as we had planned, but we did not tell them where we would be heading. The less they knew of our movements the better, as we believed that the other party faced a high risk of recapture. Since we were leaving the camp we were not required to attend the usual nightly political lecture, which had always been delivered in Chinese so our attendance had been purely for appearance sake.

We were ready to move early the next morning when we were told that there would be a delay. A number of traitors were being brought in for interrogation, there was to be no movement from the camp until they had been questioned. The accused were marched into the parade ground accompanied by a strong detachment of guerillas, some of whom we had not seen before. The two young Malays and an older Tamil man had already been knocked about. Their hands were tied behind their backs and each had a rope around his neck. They were taken to three separate locations a good distance apart and we watched as their interrogation commenced.

We already knew that there was no mercy shown to anyone believed to be working with the Japanese, but we had no idea how brutal these interrogations were. From a distance we could see that each of those being questioned was being beaten with rattan canes and that some of the inquisitors were using bayonets. The Malays were screaming out for mercy, saying that they would tell their captors whatever they wanted to know, and the Tamil was already confessing. It appeared that the two Malays had told the Japanese who was sending in food to the camps, while the Tamil had apparently made his way to a nearby kampong to see if he could find out anything that merited a reward.

All three were tied to trees for the rest of the day, and that night the political meeting was told what the traitors had confessed. It was agreed that all three would be executed the next morning and that our party could not leave until after lunch. The three condemned men were made to dig their own graves and were then put to death. A rope was wound around their neck and gradually tightened. It took some time for each of them to die and we were expected to watch. When their bodies were eventually thrown into the graves all the guerillas were happy and laughing. This only strengthened our urgent desire to quit the camp and the guerilla forces forever.

At about 2 p.m. the camp commander provided us with a guide and a package of rations for each member of our party. He also gave me a letter addressed to his Chinese contact at Pontian Ketchil and wished us luck. We were then blindfolded, a rope was passed from the guide for each of us to hold onto and we moved out slowly, one behind the other like members of a chain gang. After a while we became used to moving in this way, but it was very slow and it took us all the afternoon to reach the point where the guide told us we could remove the blindfolds. We found ourselves on the edge of another rubber plantation. The guide then said goodbye and quickly made off into the rubber.

Without wasting any time we wished the other five good luck as they moved off north. Within minutes it was as though Mac and I had never seen them or the Chinese guerillas, and once again we were masters of our own destiny.

One way of displaying this mastery, I thought, would be to arrange a little bit of trouble for the Japanese as we made our way across Malaya — sabotaging railway lines and burning anything that the Japs could use. I put this to Mac, who was all for it. In fact we reckoned we could be just as effective as the guerillas.

We were steadily making our way through the rubber trees as we discussed our plans, but would soon have to camp for the night. Near dusk we spotted a lean-to that the tappers must have used as a shelter when it rained. It was rough but it suited, so we set a small fire to heat some of the cooked rice we had been given and enjoyed a cigarette from the small supply I had built up while we were in the guerillas' camp. We felt surprisingly relaxed now we were free agents once again.

We woke early, knowing that we must eat and be on our way before the tappers moved in for the day's work. Just as we could hear the tappers in the distance we came to a pineapple plantation where we were able to hide before they got close enough to see us. The small fruit were ready to eat and, as we soon discovered, very sweet. This satisfied our craving for something tasty after the bland diet we had endured since leaving Changi, so we spent the day gorging ourselves until the acid from the fruit made our gums and lips sore. When we got home again, we decided we would celebrate Pineapple Day each year as our own personal holiday.

Feeling content and giving in to the hot balmy day, Mac and I fell asleep. However we were both soon wide awake when a group of Japanese soldiers came to pick and load a truck full of pineapples. We quickly gathered our packs, crawled to the edge of the plantation and slid into a hollow in the adjoining rubber plantation. After a noisy hour or so the Japanese were satisfied with their harvest and drove off. Once again, instinct had saved us from recapture, but we were not deterred and decided to stay close to this ready source of sugar for another day. Then we would move on further north, where we would have to cross the main road and railway joining Singapore and Kuala Lumpur.

EIGHT

Sabotage

The rubber plantation we were going through the next day was a big one and the Japanese had already got it back into production. Late in the day we sighted the administration buildings and the large factory where the latex was turned into blocks of raw rubber. The factory was well separated from the housing area, the doors were wide open and it seemed to have no special security. We carefully approached and took up a position where we could watch for any activity, but the workers had already left for their own housing lines and the manager was back in his European-style bungalow. So, leaving our packs out of sight we quietly made for the factory, which was a full of blocks of treated latex, large vats and plenty of wood and other flammable material. We also discovered several drums of oil, which we poured from one end of the building to the other, over the latex piles and timber and finally out the door. We then spread a number of bags along the trail of oil to act as a wick, set a match to it and made off into the rubber. We could see that the fire had taken hold before we got out of sight and it soon appeared to be well and truly blazing. All hell broke loose when the fire was discovered, but by this time it had hit the raw rubber and a dense black smoke was billowing into the sky. We didn't wait any longer but we reckoned that they had Buckley's chance of saving the factory. We had struck our first blow against the Japanese.

Later that night when we set up our camp and were quietly smoking a strictly rationed cigarette, we discussed the problem of finding our way to Pontian Ketchil. All we had to help us was a compass and a rudimentary map, with only few features shown. What we needed urgently was some more accurate information, especially the location of towns and villages as we were moving towards areas which were more heavily populated near the main northern highway. Our major difficulty was that most of the Chinese farmers we could trust had little idea of areas at any distance from their farms. What we needed was access to the more educated Chinese, but they were mostly in villages or small towns and it would be extremely risky for us to approach them. As well, some of the Chinese could not themselves be trusted.

Each morning we had to be up near dawn as not only did the tappers commence work early to beat the hottest part of the day, but the plantations offered very little cover. So it was always a quick breakfast and then set off to locate a patch of scrub we could hide in if necessary, or find the edge of the plantation another strip of jungle. Chinese farms were usually located along the edge of the jungle and the farmers were the most reliable sources of information and food, both of which, however, were strictly limited.

Our immediate problems were solved when we saw an old Chinese farmer using a water buffalo to plough a small patch of land near the edge of a strip of forest. He looked very frightened when we got closer, but when we spoke to him in English we could see his face change and he answered us in good clear English. We were about three miles from the main north–south road, he told us, but it would be dangerous to attempt a crossing in daylight. Convoys of trucks were constantly using the road and the Japanese had bicycle patrols between the towns. The best time to cross it would be early in the morning, at a spot where we could see a good distance in both directions. He was a little vague about the distances to any of the towns but thought that Sendai was a few miles to the north.

Our new-found friend also told us that the Japanese were continuously combing through the area, intimidating the local population against helping the guerilla forces with food or information. Most of the young men of all races had been taken away to do forced labour, especially to clean up any of the damaged rubber plantations and to try and get them back into production. A lot of work had already been done to a plantation and its factory just to the west. It would soon be back in full-scale production. Mac looked at me and I knew what he was thinking already, but first things first. The old man told us that there had been executions, many women had been raped, and that Japanese soldiers were coming through the area regularly. They listed all crops and livestock, which made it difficult to supply any food to the guerilla forces. Also, the Japanese wanted all available grain, vegetables and meat for their own army and the old Chinese man told us he was unsure that he could hide sufficient rice and other foodstuffs to support him and his wife.

The Kempi Tai (military secret police) had established a post in a nearby kampong and were taking in batches of people for interrogation. Most were tortured to disclose information about anyone helping the guerilla forces, and few of them were ever seen again. If any information was considered of particular importance, the person involved was quickly sent off under guard to Kempi Tai headquarters in Singapore for further torture and interrogation. The tactics of the Japanese were to turn brother against brother, or father against son, and whole areas were living in a state of perpetual fear. The Japanese also had a reward of 1000 Malay dollars for information on any Europeans hidden in the region, or for the capture of known guerilla soldiers. This sum represented a fortune to most of the poor villagers.

Our informant told us his name was Ah Lung and that his father and mother had migrated from southern China many years ago. He and his family had lived on this little plot of ground for the past fifty years, remote and separated from the kampong by more than a mile of rubber or jungle. The plot he had been ploughing was handkerchief-size by our standards. On the edge of the field was his small attap home with the usual pond behind it, a few chooks and geese. It was not much to show for fifty years of hard work. However, it was his castle, he was proud of it and he invited us in to share his meal.

Unlike most of the houses we had seen so far, it was scrupulously clean. There were few worldly possessions but what they had had been well looked after. Ah Lung's wife was a bent wrinkled old lady with a high-pitched voice. She spoke only a little English but was clearly determined to make us welcome and within a short time we were enjoying a bowl of vegetable soup with as much steaming rice and side dishes as we could eat. Ah Lung finished his meal before we did and sat smoking his pipe as he watched us catch up with our hunger.

Ah Lung told us he had no doubt that the British would eventually drive the Japanese out of Malaya, but that there was now a strong body of young Chinese who supported communism and who would cause great trouble. He was sure the war would last a long time, that there would be great hardship for those who survived and that many thousands of Chinese would be killed before freedom came. He was a wise old man and, sadly, most of what he said came true.

As the sun went down Ah Lung asked us to spend the night with them. There seemed little room, but he said they would make up a bed for us on the floor. We would be perfectly safe, he added, as no-one ever came into the area at night. We accepted his kindness with thanks.

When we awoke early the next morning, Ah Lung's wife had already prepared a substantial breakfast to ensure we had a good start for the day. She had also prepared a considerable amount of food for us to take with us. This must have come from their meagre stock of supplies and we were humbled by their generosity. When I asked Ah Lung if he would sell me some kerosene he quickly got me a bottle full. I had great difficulty getting him to take some Malay dollars, but I was determined that he should be able to replace what he had given us.

We all sat for a little while, unsure that we would ever meet again but enjoying each other's company. In this short time we had established a feeling that was hard to explain. It was as though they were elderly relatives we had known all our lives, and I think they thought of us as children needing help. Eventually, Ah Lung led us to the edge of his property and again warned us of the village with the Japanese Kempi Tai post.

Mac had been waiting to ask me what I wanted the kerosene for, as we had no lamp. I reminded him of the rubber plantation nearby and said it offered us an opportunity to indulge in a spot of fiery sabotage. Mac was as keen as I was to give it a go, so we got down to planning. It was all pretty simple really. According to Ah Lung, they were only getting the buildings ready, so it was unlikely anyone would be around late in the day. That should give us a good opportunity to set a decent fire in both the factory building and the manager's house. With time on our side we decided to take things easy until mid-afternoon, find a spot just inside the jungle and rest up until it was time to move. And that's just what we did. It was a hot day, our stomachs were full, and we soon dozed off.

Sometime later I awoke to find Mac snoring his head off. There was no hurry, so I let him sleep on. We could easily reach the factory area in a few hours and could afford to stay put for a while yet. I lay there thinking how yellow we had become from the lack of sunlight and the anti-malaria tablets. If it wasn't for our eyes and Mac's light hair we could almost be Chinese and might pass muster at a distance. Smoking another of our rationed cigarettes, I wondered what was going on in Changi and if our escape had encouraged others to get out and harass the Japanese. It was still hard for me to understand what had happened to the senior Australian officers who seemed to be so subservient to the Japanese, obeying their every order without question. What a gutless mob they were. I was glad Mac and I had broken away from their control. We would try in our small way to give the Japs something to worry about and try, wherever possible, to delay their attempts to get the rubber plantations going again.

I finally woke Mac up when I thought we should get ourselves organised for our second adventure in sabotage and we made off down the track. It took us several hours to locate the factory, which was in a small valley with a very neat set-up of buildings, most of which had recently been rebuilt. We waited until all sounds of activity had ceased before we moved closer to assess the situation. Leaving our packs and taking with us only the kerosene and our matches, we moved in closer still. When we were sure we had the place to ourselves we quickly moved into the factory.

There was plenty of combustible material — lots of attap, timber and shavings. The workers had started to move in the plant for handling the latex, but it had not yet been completed, so we heaped wood shavings and attap against the walls and the machinery. Then we moved on to the house. It had been hit by artillery fire during the fighting and the tile roof had been replaced with attap. Inside was a mess but much of the original furniture remained, so we pushed it into piles, brought in the attap that hadn't been used for the roof, and soon had a number of beautiful bonfires ready to light. All we had to do next was to set a sort of time fuse to allow us to get clear of the area before the blaze took hold. I soaked some curtains with kerosene and made a wick which I poked into each of the piles of furniture and attap before dousing the area with kerosene. Mac went to the factory with a wick and did the same with the rest of the kerosene. Then we lit the wicks and took off, making for the top of the rise where we could wait and see if the fires took hold. We sat and waited for what seemed an eternity, and then suddenly it happened. Both the house and the factory glowed red and started to smoke wildly. The 'phantom two' had struck once more. Unless someone came quickly there would be little left by the next day, but it was time for us to get out of the area so we headed for the jungle. It was starting to get dark so we couldn't hope to get more than a token distance in from the edge, but we felt elated and confident. We started a small fire, warmed up some of the food Ah Lung's wife had given us, enjoyed a cigarette, and talked about what we could do next to keep the enemy busy.

Next morning we searched along the edge of the jungle to see if we could find a track. Suddenly, Mac called out for me to come quickly. I made my way to Mac, who pointed to two army boxes with rope handles. He had already opened the larger one which contained four mortar shells. We soon discovered that the smaller box had two dozen hand grenades. We looked at each other our brains surging with ideas, fumbling around for uses to which we could put this find. Our first thought was that the mortar shells were a dead loss, but then an idea came to me. We were going to cross the railway line before long. Maybe we could place the shells against the rails in such a manner that the train would detonate them. The grenades could be used to create problems in a multitude of ways.

The important thing was for us to turn this find to maximum use, but in such a way that we would not be suspected of involvement if we were ever caught. Mac and I had made an agreement that we would never travel armed, as if we were ever caught we would be instantly classed as guerilla fighters and executed on the spot. Despite this resolve we decided to take two mortar shells with us, along with a dozen grenades. We would hide the rest under a thick bush, available for later use.

It was clumsy work carrying the ammunition box through the jungle but we stumbled on a track which took us in a north-easterly direction. It soon started to twist and turn but it seemed to maintain a northern direction and we could manage the ammunition box better. The track did not seem to have been used much and the jungle was reclaiming part of it, but after a couple of hours we found ourselves once more on the edge of the north side of the jungle, not far from the start of yet another rubber plantation which seemed well back into production. Now we were in a quandary. To take the ammunition box with us, would limit our ability to move quickly and force us to travel close together. After a brief discussion we decided to hide the box in thick bush at the edge of the jungle and to take a mortar shell and two grenades each. I didn't dare mark any trees as the tappers would surely report it to the manager and now that we were saboteurs we were doubly anxious to keep our presence from them.

We would have liked to take a crack at the factory on this property, but our main objective was the railway line, so we headed west, towards it. When we were within earshot of the line we decided to stop for the night. We still had a lot to discuss and to plan — in particular, the means by which we would safely hide the shells yet be absolutely sure they would detonate. Mac suggested we should put a hand grenade with the pin out beside the shells. We could hold the lever down with a stake. If the shells were not detonated by the train, the grenade would probably set them off. It seemed a wise precaution to ensure success. We had already agreed that we would not, if possible, undertake any sabotage which might take innocent lives. However, derailing a train and damaging a section of rail constituted major sabotage and we must just hope that no one was injured.

Next morning we approached the train line with great caution. It was well we did, because we soon heard a train approaching from the south, heading towards Kuala Lumpur. It was a goods train with a carriage full of Japanese soldiers at the rear. After it had passed we made our way parallel to the line, looking for a suitable area to set up our attack. We needed a raised section of bank so that the train would go down an embankment and turn over when it left the line. Hopefully it would also tear up a section of the track. We didn't have to go very far before we reached an ideal spot. Not only was there a raised section of track where it passed across a gully but there was good scrub cover if we had to hide, and the whole area was screened from the rubber by a wide patch of scrub and undergrowth. Leaving our packs in the scrub, we crawled up the bank to the line to see what we were faced with. While I started scraping a hole on the inside of the right line, Mac went down and got the two shells. He was just starting to climb back up the bank when I heard the distant rumble of a train coming from the direction of Kuala Lumpur. This time it had a large number of platform cars carrying a variety of army vehicles, ammunition and stores. Just the sort of train we would like to derail. The engine had two soldiers riding on the front, looking for any obstructions or damage to the rails, and the rear carriage was again full of soldiers, so we knew what we were up against. So long as we camouflaged the shells with a leafy branch it was most unlikely that the guards would see anything before it was too late. While we waited for the train to get out of sight, Mac cut a small stake to hold the handle of the grenade in place.

Taking the shells up the bank with us, we dug out enough of the metal around the sleepers to get the shells nearly level with the line. We placed a rock under the nose of each shell to ensure that the detonator was struck with enough force to explode the shells, then packed the grenade beside the line, with the small stake holding the lever in place. Finally, we placed a small leafy branch on top of our handiwork. Our work was complete but sadly, we were not around to witness the successful conclusion as we didn't dare stay nearby. The Japanese would immediately sweep the area, looking for guerillas, but we would be long gone, hopefully planning another upset for the enemy.

This time we headed north-east through the edge of the rubber, gradually placing more distance between us and the railway. We found a patch of rubber that had been let go and seemed safe from any chance encounter with tappers, so we settled down near a small creek for the remainder of the day. We had ample water to wash and shave, make a billy of tea and prepare a meal, after which we smoked another cigarette. What more could a loose POW want?

As we smoked and chattered I wondered how many of those we knew had escaped into the jungle. There seemed no way the Japanese could hold 90 000 prisoners in Changi with that lousy fence no towers or search lights and those dopey Sikh guards. However, Mac was more sceptical, and with good reason as it turned out. He reckoned a lot of the POWs seemed content to sit the war out.

Little did we know, as we sat and discussed Changi, that we were the sole escapees and that there would never be any organised harassment of the Japanese. It would be left to individual soldiers out on working parties to do what they could while someone distracted the guards. Remember that these parties were soldiers only; the officers remained in Changi. There were many documented cases of sabotage by troops outside the camps, but sadly there is no evidence of any attempt to organise sabotage from within Changi itself or to harass the enemy troops in any way. It seemed that the official position was that the war was over for those who had become POWs, and those who could have set an example were more concerned with their contract bridge scores than making any further contribution to the war effort. I was to learn a lot about this situation when I was finally returned to Changi.

We were still on the east of the railway line which we would soon have to cross. But we needed to get further north first, and top up our rations if possible. Once we crossed the rail we would be in a more settled area close to the main Singapore to Kuala Lumpur road, where there were fewer Chinese farmers. Also our friend Ah Lung had warned us that the Japanese had been using forced labour to clear a wide swathe of the bush and trees for 100 feet or so on either side of the highway as a protection against guerilla attacks.

The next morning we set off again through the old rubber area, looking for a Chinese farm. The weather, which had been surprisingly good, now took a turn for the worse. Heavy clouds formed and we could hear thunder in the north, so we started looking for temporary shelter. Luck's as good as a fortune, they say, and we soon saw ahead of us a Chinese farmer's small house. A startled Chinese man met us at the back of the house, but he recognised us as Australian soldiers, and, greeting us with a smile and a handshake, immediately asked us inside. He was old but well cared for and spoke very good English. The storm had now arrived in earnest — lightning, thunder and violent wind with very heavy rain pelting down. Once we were inside, the farmer's wife greeted us, also in perfect English. It turned out they had both been school teachers before the war and had decided to spend their last days on this small farm, which they told us was quite close to civilisation. There was a small town only a few miles to the east which supplied them with all their requirements. Their house was cleaner and more comfortably appointed than any of the other farms we had been in. They had better furniture and a few useful modern aids, such as a wood stove and running water from the tank which had a galvanised-iron roof, which was unusual in this part of Malaya.

The farmer introduced his wife as Ying and told us to call him Harry. They knew we would be hungry so Ying prepared a meal for us as the storm lashed the house, sometimes making conversation difficult. Harry was keen to hear how we had escaped from Changi. He was quite familiar with the area and chuckled as we told him of our adventures to date and our harassment of the Japanese. The guerilla forces had not yet approached him for food or supplies. Harry went on to say that while he would help anyone who was opposed to the Japanese, he would not support Chinese communism. He was strongly in favour of democracy, but said that the young Chinese students were very anti-British and pro-communist, though he didn't think they would remain that way if they ever had to live in a communist state. However, university students seemed to be troublesome the world over, Harry observed. When we told Ying and Harry about Chin Peng, Harry said he knew quite a bit about him already and felt the world would hear much more about him later. How right he was.

Meanwhile, Ying had made a fine meal for us all. There was as much food as we could eat and lashings of hot tea. We all sat around after this feast, and enjoyed one of our cigarettes as Mac and I talked about our lives in Australia and our hosts told us about their young life in Yong Peng, where they both grew up, their education and their careers as teachers. As time wore on the storm gradually passed over and we were able to wash our dirty clothing, shave and generally make ourselves presentable again. Harry said we should spend another day at his home and he would give us full details of the area, the location of the Japanese troops, and advice on the best way and place for us to cross both the railway and the main road. He could also fill in information on our map to help us make our way to Pontian Ketchil. This was just the sort of assistance we needed.

At about 10 the next morning Harry took his bike down to a small village about a mile away to buy several items that we needed. He also wanted to catch up on the latest gossip and find out if there was any news of a railway accident. We asked Harry to get us some matches, kerosene and cigarettes, and some rice. While he was away we cleaned up the remainder of our gear. Harry arrived back shortly after midday with all the items and full of news. Yes, there had been a derailment. An engine and three wagons had gone down the embankment, quite a bit of rail was torn up and, best of all, the wagons had caught fire as one of them had been carrying drums of fuel. The guerillas were being blamed.

We spent the remainder of the day getting information from Harry on the route we should take and plotting it on our map. At the same time we had to be careful to ensure that no-one other than us would be able to understand the markings we used. We had no intention of writing anything that would lead anyone else along our route, or allow them to backtrack to those who helped us. The immediate area was not well covered by the Japanese, Harry told us, so it was a good time to cross the line and the road. Harry had a small ancient radio that was able to get local reception and also the station in Singapore, but naturally the news and the music were Japanese oriented. They claimed victories in New Guinea and over the American Navy, that they were bombing Australia and would soon invade New Zealand.

We didn't believe them any more than Harry did, but it gave us plenty to talk about that night.

Next morning, after a leisurely breakfast, we carefully packed our kits. We had enough food to last us for two weeks, so long as we were careful and supplemented our supplies with any fruit we could scrounge on the way. Harry and Ying had not hesitated to give us whatever they had and we were all saddened by our leave taking. If we survived and the war ended in a reasonable time, Mac and I planned to revisit these gentle folk.

NINE

Scratch two Japanese

Our plans now called for us to make our way north for about five miles, swing west to cross the railway in an uninhabited area, and then move slightly north to cross the main road at a spot where a long straight stretch would help us see anything coming from a distance. This was most important, as trees had been felled in a wide strip either side of the road. The weather was fine but very hot and as we trudged along the sweat poured off us. The rubber we passed had been neglected but there were signs that it was being brought back into production.

We were approaching a dirt road when we heard a vehicle approaching, so we slumped down behind a tree and watched as a small army truck slowly drew near. There were two Japanese inside, both armed with revolvers, and they seemed to be looking for something. They passed us and stopped about a 100 yards down the road where both men got out and set off towards a rise about half a mile away. This might be the time to use one of the grenades we were carrying. I had told Mac earlier of my plan to remove the pin from a grenade and wedge it under the clutch pedal of a truck or van. When the driver started the engine and depressed the clutch he would dislodge the grenade. Four seconds later he would join his ancestors and the vehicle would be wrecked. This seemed like an ideal opportunity to test the plan as Mac could keep an eye on the two Japanese while I shot over to the vehicle and effectively booby-trapped it.

Everything went as planned. It was a soda to put the grenade in place and I was back with Mac very smartly. The two Japanese, who I think were from a construction unit, were still at the rise as we moved back deeper into the rubber, lay down and waited for their return. After about twenty minutes they slowly made their way back to their truck. The passenger got in first, and then the driver. They sat and talked for a while before the driver started the engine. A few seconds later there was a loud detonation and a lot of smoke, followed by a second explosion as the petrol tank blew up. The occupants didn't know what hit them. While we knew that the soldiers would be killed, we hadn't imagined the vehicle blowing up at the same time and Mac and I beat a very hasty retreat.

As we started north again we were both very silent, not at all sure that this was what we had wanted to happen. Taking life was something I was not too well prepared for, and nor was Mac. It was one thing to shoot at someone who was trying to kill you, but to kill the way we had just done was another thing altogether. I knew we would have to talk about this before we did it again.

Before I had a chance to raise the subject we

heard a noise ahead, so made our way carefully towards what turned out to be a small village in a shallow valley. There appeared to be about twenty houses and it was a typical Malay kampong except that there was one house with a flagpole flying a Japanese flag. As we watched from a safe distance we saw several Japanese soldiers, most of whom were in a relaxed state, without shirts. This was unusual and meant that there was no officer or NCO with them. We would have liked to disturb their leisure, but not knowing if there were other soldiers nearby we decided to give them a miss.

We continued on our way, stopping later to make ourselves a meal when we were satisfied that the Tamil rubber tappers had finished their work for the day. Mac and I sensed another opportunity for sabotage. We soon came across a wide track which led us to a rubber processing factory and a number of other buildings. The manager's house was far enough from the factory for us to start another fire in comparative safety. The factory building was made of brick, but there was plenty of combustible material lying around. All was quiet and again we gathered fuel and doused the area with some of the kerosene that Harry had bought for us. We were not disturbed and, setting a long wick alight, we made off into the rubber to await the result. Once again, the fire took hold rapidly and it seemed a long time before the occupants of the manager's house woke up to what was happening.

Had there been an organised force moving around the plantations, they could easily have set back the production of rubber and made the Japanese deploy a lot of soldiers to protect the factories. Mac and I were demonstrating what could be done. The strips of jungle between plantations made it easy to hit and run, and to hit the Japanese where it hurt most. It was a pity that the seat-warmers in Changi hadn't the gumption to create small parties to sabotage the Japanese in lower Malaya.

The sun was setting as we looked for a safe place to spend the night. It would soon be dark, so we selected a spot on a small rise that would allow us a good view of anyone approaching. I dug a hole and made a fire to heat our meal and to boil the billy. We were getting pretty short of water so would have to find a stream the next day. The smoke from our fire kept the mozzies at bay as we sat and ate our meal, quietly talking about our approach to the railway line the next day. The Japanese would have increased security against further attacks. It would have been nice to create some more havoc, but we agreed that we should concentrate on getting across the line without being seen. Further sabotage would have to wait.

Mac woke me at dawn with a cup of billy tea and we were soon on our way. The main railway line was only about a mile away. Luckily for us, the ground was undulating and we were able to reach a spot fairly close to the rail where we could see how much traffic was using the line. Nothing happened for about half an hour and then a train approached from the south. It was half and half goods wagons and carriages, the last one filled with soldiers. The train moved onto a side track we had not noticed. This was a spur line that led off to the east, complete with a signal pole and a box where the point mechanism was located.

After the train had disappeared from view we waited another quarter of an hour and a goods train with a number of oil tankers came in the opposite direction. It too had the usual guards on the engine and at the back. Before long we heard another south-bound train approaching. This time it was a troop train of about ten carriages and we let it get out of earshot before we cautiously made our way down to the line. All seemed quiet, so Mac suggested we lodge one of the grenades in the thin part of the points and put another in the points box for good measure. If we pulled the pins and saw that the lever was held down we may yet be able to cause another derailment. We got to work immediately and then moved on. We hadn't got too far before we heard two explosions, but we never discovered the extent of the damage we had caused.

We were now entering a region where few Chinese had land. Any houses we struck from now on would most likely be those of Malays and Indians, so if we heard any sounds of human habitation we promptly changed direction. Because of the build up of population we had to do this so often it became difficult to maintain a sense of direction. We still had our compass, however, and we kept returning to our westerly course. We both felt tense and edgy and needed to have a few hours rest before we even considered approaching the main road. The rubber we were in was overgrown and had apparently been let go, so we were able to find a secure hideout for the remainder of the day.

The next morning we headed for the main road. We were not yet close enough to hear any noise so we pushed on at a good pace, only slowing down when we finally heard the noise of traffic. We reckoned that the traffic would probably be lightest in the late afternoon, as most natives were back in their homes by about five o'clock. The other alternative was early in the morning. But first of all we had to get as close as possible to the road and observe what was happening and how much traffic there really was. We crawled the last 100 yards on our stomachs, working our way towards a piece of ground that was about six feet above the road. When we made it to the edge we were surprised to see that we had not arrived at a long straight stretch of road. We could only see the approaching traffic for about a 100 yards on either side. The trees had been felled on the opposite side of the road, but because of their foliage they lay at rest about four or five feet above the ground. This meant we would have to walk along the trunks of the trees, jumping from one to the next until we reached the edge of the rubber. This would make it very difficult to duck out of view if any traffic approached.

Quite apart from these difficulties, we were amazed at the continuous flow of traffic. If it wasn't Japanese trucks it was Malays and Indians on bikes or in carts. There were also a lot of motorcycles. We lay by the road and watched as the afternoon passed, and still the traffic flowed. I had hoped that it would cease before sundown but it was not to be. Darkness fell. There was no way we could cross once the light faded, as we had no hope of negotiating the tree trunks in the dark, and the headlights of approaching vehicles would show us up clearly. This meant we had to spend the night where we were and be ready to move at first light, in the hope that there was less traffic. As dawn broke, the road seemed quiet and peaceful. However, we decided that we should make the crossing one at a time.

Mac moved off first. He seemed to reach the fallen trees in next to no time and I took heart at his success. There had been no movement on the road up to this point but I waited until Mac was about halfway along the tree trunks before I crawled to the edge of the bank. Just as I leaned forward to jump, two Japanese soldiers on bikes rode underneath me, peddling fairly fast. Unfortunately I had leaned too far forward to stop myself jumping down. I landed about thirty feet behind the soldiers but they didn't seem to hear me and I was able to get across the road and onto the tree trunks before one of them realised that something had moved behind him. By the time they had turned around, dropped their bikes and unslung their rifles I was about three quarters of the way across the tree trunks. They both fired at me but missed. Mind you, I wasn't much of a target jumping from trunk to trunk, and by the time they got off their third shot I was into the rubber. Mac and I pushed on into the plantation at speed. The soldiers continued firing but they got nowhere near us.

We didn't stop until we reached the far edge of the plantation, where the jungle started again. Neither of us believed that the soldiers would attempt to follow us, but the bad side was that they would report what had happened and the Japanese would now know that there were two Australian soldiers loose in the area. I suggested to Mac that we change our direction and go north for a while, away from the area where the Japanese would expect to find us. It involved extra travelling but seemed our safest option.

We were on the edge of a strip of jungle, so had to search for a track or a way in. Mac found one nearby, and as it headed nearly due north we took it. From its appearance the path hadn't been used much for a long time so we felt reasonably safe and made good progress until we reached a spot where the track was crossed by two others. We took the path that led north-west and, more through good luck than good management, we soon came to a small bubbling creek where we washed out some dirty clothes, boiled some water for our water bottles, and prepared a meal. The big problem was that our friends, the leeches, quickly found us and we were forced to pack up and move on. About two hours later we reached the edge of another strip of jungle. In front of us lay another plantation, but this one was for palm oil. It was not a pleasant area to move through as we knew that palm oil plantations had a lot of low scrub and were supposed to be full of snakes. However, we were where we were and had to make the best we could of it.

Now that we had been sighted by the Japanese we agreed that we'd have to put sabotage on hold. We would be blamed for anything that occurred for miles and didn't want to make any waves in what we knew was our critical location. The best thing we could do was return to the edge of the jungle where we could make a hide, cook a meal and set ourselves up for the night. We did all this and were just settling down to rest when we were startled by some very loud growling not too far away. It must have been a tiger, as no other native animal would be so loud, but there wasn't much we could do about it other than hope it wasn't coming our way. We heard the growling several more times but the animal was clearly moving away from us. That was as close as we ever got to a tiger. In fact we had been very lucky so far, as there were also many poisonous snakes in Malaya but we hadn't encountered any. It was people who were our main concern.

At about this time I realised that I had lost the wristwatch my darling wife had given me before we left Australia. It was a gold Rolex, for which she had paid a lot of money, and I was very upset. It probably came off when I was under pressure trying to cross the trees while the soldiers were firing at me. Fortunately, Mac had his watch so we were still able to know the time. At any rate, we now had to rechart our course and head for the west coast. The palm oil plantation seemed to go on for ever. It was dirty, the undergrowth was a constant source of annoyance, and it took us many hours to reach its far side. We found ourselves in an area that had previously been cleared but the jungle was rapidly reclaiming the ground, which made our progress even slower. When we hit a path running from north to south we were so fed up we decided to take it and see what turned up. The scrub soon thinned out and we entered an area that showed signs of habitation. Then, ahead of us we sighted a food stall where a number of tracks converged.

We stopped. Should we go on? We badly needed to know our location and how far we were from the coast. Our map indicated that there should be a canal near here and if we could find it we would know we were close to Pontian Ketchil. Then at last we could try to get help with a junk and sail to Ceylon. After some discussion Mac and I decided we would take the risk of talking to the stallholder and try in a roundabout way to discover if the canal was nearby. We walked up to find a young Malay who showed no signs of surprise and produced two glasses of coloured lolly water for which we paid in Malay dollars.

These small roadside stalls are found all over Malaya, and are a gathering spot for the locals for a snack and to hear the latest gossip. However, we weren't locals and we were very careful how we approached the subject of just where we were. We asked the way to Pontein Besar, and if there was also a canal. The young Malay told us that Pontein Besar, was on the track we had come down and that there was a canal that led to Pontian Ketchil about a half mile away. Feeling we had been pretty smart getting the information we wanted while misleading our informant about where we were heading, we bade him goodbye and retraced our way back along the track.

As soon as we were around a bend we left the track and made a half-circle around behind the food stall. As we did we came close to the start of the canal, but there were lots of Malay houses on either side and we needed to stop and have a good recce of the area before we looked for the Chinese merchant. I had memorised his name as it was far too dangerous to have anything written down that could link him with the guerilla forces. Even the note the camp commandant had written was addressed to 'River' and signed 'House'. And all it said, in English, was 'Please help my friends'.

TEN

Betrayal

We crossed into some thick scrub and set up camp about 200 yards south of the canal. We appeared to be quite safe and Mac started to get some food ready while I went off in search of water. I carefully made my way down to a creek which ran into the canal, filled the water bottles and made my way back towards the camp. I was about fifty yards away when Mac called out loudly, 'Penny, I am surrounded by Malays and Indians and they are all armed'. When I looked around I saw a group of about sixty Malays and Indians closing in on me. They were armed with knives, axes and lengths of timber. There was no way we could possibly get away.

Our captors started to shout at us all at once, then pushed us together quickly and tied us up with rope. Then they started to brawl amongst themselves over our few possessions. This was to our advantage, as it happened, as everything was thrown about. The map disappeared, the letter blew away, and each of the natives took anything that they fancied. Then they argued what to do with us. The Indians were all for killing us on the spot and handing our bodies over to the Japanese, but the Malays said that we were worth a lot more alive. It was agreed that we would be taken into Pontian Ketchil and handed over to the Malay police, who would notify the Japanese and collect the reward for the villagers.

The crowd had grown as this discussion took place and we were being kicked and punched, even urinated on. The mob was really enjoying the spectacle of the degradation of the two Europeans and we were kicked along down the road to Pontian Ketchil. Even the woman spat on us and we were soon black and blue from the kicks and the beating we received. Someone went off and alerted the local police, who locked us up in a tiny dirty cell.

At last Mac and I could talk to each other. We had to stick to our cover story through thick and thin if we were to escape being beheaded, so we carefully went over what we were going to tell the Japanese when they arrived. Our story was that we were members of the 2/29th Battalion who had been left behind in the fighting. We couldn't say that we belonged to the 2/4th as they had not fought on the peninsula. We would say that we had had been lost in the jungle for some time and had survived on pineapples, tapioca root and caught birds. Under no circumstances were we to let on that we'd had any contact with the Chinese or had even heard of the guerilla forces.

We spoke very quietly, leaning in close to each other, as the police had told us that they would beat us up if we talked. However, they were not very smart since they had other empty cells and could easily have separated us. One of the police came in with a bottle of water and gave us each a drink. Meanwhile, the mob who had caught us remained outside the police station, not wanting to go home until they saw the Japanese take us away and they knew their reward would be forthcoming. Well, they didn't have too long to wait. The cell door was opened and we were taken out and handed over to two Japanese soldiers, taken out to their truck, and told to get in the back. So far, so good. Both the police and these two soldiers had treated us reasonably. We drove for some time before arriving at Johore Bahru, where we were handed over to members of the Kempi Tai.

How suddenly things were to change! The Kempi Tai was the Imperial Japanese Army's secret police and they were feared even by their own people. They were answerable to no-one but their own senior officers and were the masters of torture. No-one could teach them any new way to extract information, true or false. They always got a confession.

ELEVEN

Kempi Tai HQ Johore Bahru

We were stripped, checked to see that we had nothing useful, screamed at as we had no idea what they were saying to us, and beaten with rifles and swords. Once we had our clothes back on we were handcuffed, placed in leg irons, and our hands and legs were chained and locked. We tumbled into a cage-like bare cell with a high barred window and a mesh fence across the front. It was filthy from the previous occupants, whose excrement and blood covered the floor and walls. We had no doubt what we were in for. We were told to sit on the floor with our legs bent in front of us and left alone except for a guard who sat nearby, facing us to see that we didn't move or attempt to talk to each other.

And so we sat through the rest of the day. We had no food, no water, and not much hope. Through that first night we went through the pangs of fear of what was going to happen to us. We itched from the bites of the millions of bugs that lived here, and feasted on our blood. And we couldn't even scratch them off.

After a sleepless night, the guard yelled at us to keep us awake even longer. It was part of the softening-up process, to prepare us for the questioning ahead. At some stage I was taken down a passageway and into a small room where a Japanese officer sat at a table. I was pushed into a chair and the officer, who spoke fair English, started to ask me questions. He seemed quite mild mannered and we started with what seemed stupid questions such as my mother's and father's names, what he did for a living, and where he was born. This all seemed simple enough and I answered with a certain amount of truth. Then we moved on to my time in the army. I gave the usual answer — name and army number — but this went over like a lead balloon and suddenly everything changed. The officer came around and struck me across the back with his sword, which was still in its scabbard. When I fell to the floor the sergeant who was the only other person in the room kicked me hard in the back. Both men screamed at me in Japanese and I was thrown back onto the chair. The officer resumed his seat and calmly asked me the same set of questions once again. When I gave the same answer the sergeant kicked the chair from under me and started to kick me hard in the crotch, which caused me to black out for a few seconds. Then he started kicking me in the stomach and head. My nose and mouth were bleeding as I was put back on the chair and the same questions were repeated. I wasn't going to give in that easily, but the two men beat me so severely that I became unconscious and was apparently dragged back to the cell and thrown in.

This was used as a warning to Mac, who was taken out to the same room where he apparently went through the same questioning ... with the same result. We both regained conscious at about the same time.

We were bruised and battered, and filthy from our own urine and blood. Still defiant, we whispered some words of encouragement to each other. At least the chain between our legs and hands had been removed. We were both very thirsty but when I croakingly asked the guard for a drink he just laughed. There was no way they were going to give us anything until we answered their questions, and seeing that they had no intention of letting us go to a toilet, I suppose it was better that we had none. This time the guard let us doze off, and so our first day with the Kempi Tai passed. There was little Mac or I could say to each other as we needed to conserve whatever strength we had for the next day, when we knew things would get even tougher. All we could think about was how we would get through the day. I slept fitfully but at least got a few hours sleep. The bugs swarmed over us and we had still been given no food or water.

Next day we awoke to hear the town of Johore Bahru coming to life, and the guard changed. This time we got an absolute stinker who really let us know what he thought of us. He yelled and then kicked us for not obeying his commands. We had to sit up straight and not even look at each other. After several hours Mac was taken out to start the day's torture. Fortunately the interrogation room was far enough away for me to not hear what they were doing to him but after about two hours he was dragged back into the cell and thrown in the corner. He was a mass of blood and seemed to be bleeding from many parts of his body but the guard wouldn't let me go over to him. Anyway it was my turn now and I was taken down the corridor to the same room where the same officer sat drinking a cup of coffee. He asked me if I would like one and naturally enough I said yes. He sent a soldier out to bring one to me, but it was placed on the table out of my reach. Once I had answered his questions I could have it, I was told, and we immediately went back to the previous day's questions about my army experience. When I answered again with my name and number, they really let me have it.

They had brought in a baseball bat and several rattan canes about half an inch in diameter. One of my tormentors used a baseball bat and the other a cane as they beat me thoroughly. The bat broke the skin and the cane started the blood flowing. When I passed out, they threw a bucket of water over me to bring me around and sat me back on the chair again, looping my arms over the back of the chair so I wouldn't fall off. 'You will answer all my questions', the officer said, 'or you will die. There is no way out. The Kempi Tai always gets answers to its questions, so take my advice. If you want to live, start talking'. He resumed drinking his cup of coffee and the sergeant calmly started drinking the one that had supposedly been for me. I was in a pitiful state. Blood was seeping through my shorts and shirt and I didn't know how many different wounds I now had. I had urinated several times in the agony of the beating and my pants were filthy where I had lost control. After they finished their coffee, the questions were repeated. My answers were unchanged so they laid me across the table and used rattan canes to beat me unconscious. I awoke back in the cell with Mac, who was beside himself at my condition, even though his was little better.

We both wondered how long we could stand this punishment without water and food. The new guard was not very interested in us and seemed a bit dopey anyway, so we were able to whisper to each other without him noticing. After a while I asked Mac whether we should be prepared to give out some of the information they wanted and just how much he thought it was safe to reveal at this stage. I told Mac I could hold on if he could, but it was up to him to say when he had taken enough. Our problem was that we knew this was only a branch of the Kempi Tai, which had its headquarters in Singapore, and I was certain we would be handed over to them before long. So should we give a bit more information? If we satisfied them that we were as we said we were — that is, soldiers left behind during the fighting on the peninsula — we would probably be sent back to a POW camp.

On the third morning I was taken to another room where a captain sat at the table. Through an interpreter, he wasted no time. 'We need answers from you that will confirm that you are just two soldiers left from the fighting. Otherwise we will assume that you are spies and you will be executed. It is up to you, but we are not prepared to waste any more time.'

With this he left the room and I was taken back to Mac. Our shackles were taken off and we were given water and some rice and vegetables. Mac wanted to know what had brought on the change. I told him I thought they were puzzled by our determination not to answer their questions and suggested we should now answer anything they asked providing it didn't hurt anyone else and kept to the story we had agreed on. Lets seem very reluctant, I added but appear frightened of being executed. Let them think they have forced us into talking.

At mid afternoon I was taken off for questioning once again. I think I put on a good impersonation of a frightened man. The questions covered how we had spent the time between the fighting and our capture, and my answers were carefully written down by a clerk. I was returned to the cell and Mac was taken off to see if his story tallied with mine. He was returned without the officer making any comment. Mac and I were confident that we had put on a good performance, but with these highly unpredictable people we couldn't be sure of what would happen next.

The guard seemed to treat us better than previously. He brought us water and an old piece of towel, for which we were very grateful, and a bucket we could use as a toilet. We spent the rest of the day cleaning ourselves as best we could, and that night we were given a meal of rice and vegetables with a small roll. We were both very hungry and the food disappeared very quickly. Even though we were black and blue from the beatings, we still both managed to have a decent sleep.

The next morning we were taken out together to a courtyard where there was a large concrete trough full of water. We were given a lump of soap and a safety razor and told to shave and wash all over. These instructions were all in Japanese, with suitable actions showing what they wanted. We shaved each other as we had no mirror, bathed and were given some shorts and shirts. We looked and felt like new men and hoped that we were not being made ready for execution.

We were taken to the front of the building where our hands were tied behind our backs and we were loaded onto a small truck, which took us through Johore Bahru and across the Causeway to Singapore Island which had been renamed Shonan. The truck continued out towards Changi and we believed that we were being returned to the POW camp, but we stopped on the perimeter of the camp and were delivered to the headquarters of the Sikh guards. An Indian officer signed for us and we were placed in a wire cage about five feet high and eight by six feet across. It was smaller than most dog pens and, worse than that, it was in the open with no shade. The Indians promptly placed a guard on us who showed his hatred immediately by spitting on us both and drawing his hand across his throat. We were in for a torrid time.

The guard was changed regularly and each one found some way to humiliate us. None of them let us have any water, although one urinated on us indicating that we could drink that. I don't think I have ever hated people as much as I hated these Sikhs, who were traitors anyway having gone over to the Japanese after the fall of Singapore. It had been a long day and we were puzzled by what was going on. Were we to be released, or were we being held here for execution? The attitude of the guards seemed to indicate the latter, but as the sun went down an Indian captain came out and told the guard to release us into his charge. The guard was told to wait outside the officer's hut and we were taken inside, the captain told us to not speak loudly as he didn't want anyone to hear what was said.

Then he quietly told us that he had agreed to join the group led by Chandra Bose, who was supporting the Japanese against the British, as that way he was able to protect as many of his own people as he could. Those who had refused to change sides were being killed and starved. The captain could help us at night but not during the day, as the Japanese must not know what he was doing or he would join us in the cage. The guards, he told us were bad news, they were very bad elements within the Sikh nation, and we would have to handle them the best way we could. At least he could feed us and give us water at night while we remained here, but he had no idea what was to happen to us as the matter was in the hands of the Kempi Tai in Singapore. He then gave us a good helping of curry and rice with as much tea as we could drink, and a cigarette each which we had to smoke before we left the hut. At least we had a friend here, but he had to play a double game, and it was up to us to see we didn't let him down.

We slept fitfully. Not only were we uncertain of our future, but the mozzies woke us if we did nod off. Next morning we were given a small ball of rice and a mug of water, which was all we received that day. There was another guard on duty that night, but the captain took us into his hut once again and fed us. He also told us that he had been advised we were to be picked up the next day. He didn't know where we were going, but suggested we eat well as no-one knew what the future held.

TWELVE

Kempi Tai HQ Singapore

The next morning we received a bowl of rice and a mug of water. About an hour later, a small truck arrived and we were handed over to two Japanese soldiers and an officer. They promptly handcuffed us and put us in the back of the truck with an armed guard to keep us company. Then we set off back towards Singapore and pulled up outside a building with the letters YMCA, still visible on the front. We had arrived at Kempi Tai headquarters for the area. Thousands of people went through here, we later learned, but only a few lived to tell of the experience.

We were shoved down a passageway to a caged-off area about forty feet by twenty with mesh wire across the front and crammed with men, women and children of all races. This was the holding pen for those awaiting questioning and we were warned not to talk to anyone. What followed was a nightmare. The floors above were interrogation rooms and we could hear people screaming and being screamed at. The pen had a dozen or so women, some Eurasian but mostly Chinese, all of whom were very frightened, a number of children aged from about ten to sixteen, and about thirty men of all ages — Chinese, a few Indians, some Eurasians, and two Europeans, one of whom was the Church of England Bishop of Singapore. There were about four buckets to be used as toilets, with no privacy for the women and children, but whenever they used them several others made a body screen for them.

It was a soul-destroying situation for everyone in this pen and we set ourselves down next to the Bishop, who quietly told us what to expect. All the while, guards were coming into the pen and taking out various people. When prisoners were returned to the pen, few were conscious and all were bleeding from cuts to their nose or mouth. They were just thrown in, but some men or women would immediately drag them back to a wall and do what they could for them. Some of our fellow prisoners had already had a lot of punishment, while others such as ourselves had yet to face the full force of the inquisition.

The cage became a madhouse as the day wore on. The noise and screams from the interrogation rooms had the women and children scared to death and we men weren't too brave either. There was no respite as someone was always being taken out and bodies were being thrown back in all day. Some of the punishment was unbelievable. A number of the older Chinese men had lost most of their fingernails and toenails, which had been ripped out with pliers. Others had had slivers of bamboo driven under the nails. We also learnt that the Japanese were using what was known as the water torture — a hose or funnel was pushed down your throat and the water turned on. When your stomach was distended almost to bursting point, they beat it with canes. Another Chinese man told us that they were applying electrodes to all the sensitive parts of the body, especially the genitals. Apparently people only left here after signing a confession or on a stretcher, dead.

Several times every hour a guard or an officer would come into the pen and look over all those incarcerated, sometimes asking them their name but often just to beat someone up. Every time the guards spotted anyone talking they came in and beat the offenders for as long as it took them to get rid of their bile. Mac and I seemed to be prime targets and on our first day we received attention from every new guard as well as several senior NCOs and officers who came in for various reasons. I managed a whispered conversation with the Bishop, who had yet to be taken out for questioning. He told me he was charged with inciting rebellion. It was a trumped-up charge based on allegations from some Indian workers no doubt seeking favours from the Japanese. He had been taken from the internees' camp to the YMCA Building three days ago.

Later on when the interrogators had finished for the day, a ball of rice was given to each person and two buckets of hot tea were provided for the forty-four persons incarcerated. Some were too far gone to eat, though their friends encouraged them to do so. When the new guards came on duty they immediately started to beat up anyone who failed to bow sufficiently low to them. Even the children received kicks or blows. With the noise now stopped from upstairs it was not possible for anyone to talk without the guards hearing, so we were left alone with our thoughts.

The next morning one of the first persons taken out was the Bishop, followed by several women and children. Then it was the turn of two of the Eurasians. Soon the volume of noise from above increased. We could clearly hear some of the women and children screaming and it was some hours before the first of them were returned. Amongst them were two women, both bleeding extensively from the mouth. They had been badly beaten and one had her clothes torn. We all thought she had been raped, but later found out she had had electrodes applied to her vagina. Apparently she was accused of helping hide a Chinese youth wanted by the Kempi Tai and she was taken out day after day until she eventually died, without disclosing his whereabouts. She was a very brave lady. When the Bishop came back he was bleeding from the nose and mouth and had been savagely beaten for not admitting he was inciting rebellion. His hands were also bloody from where he had been struck with a lump of wood.

More of the inmates were taken upstairs during the day. Mac and I expected we would soon join them, but it was not to be. We sat in this pen for another two days doing all we could to help those being thrown back, mostly in an unconscious state. Even this was extremely dangerous as the guards usually came in if they saw you trying to revive an unconscious victim and either beat you up or kicked them unmercifully. So even helping fellow prisoners could bring them into further trouble.

Few people realise the full extent of the power that the Kempi Tai had over the Japanese themselves. They were not subject to any civilian law; they had their own goals; they tried people in military courts where there was no right to appeal; they conducted their inquiries within their own building; and their own doctors provided death certificates as required. It is easy then, to understand the power they wielded throughout any area under Japanese control. They were bought in whenever a commander failed in obtaining his objective. Their methods of interrogation encompassed every form of torture known to man and they boasted that they always had a confession when they put an offender before an army court.

I knew my agony was about to begin when my name was called and I was led out by an armed guard who took me upstairs to a small cell with a table and two chairs. It was here that I first met Sergeant Koshi Amura. He had served in the Kempi Tai for fifteen years in various locations and had recently been transferred to Singapore from Manchuria. Short and stocky and extremely ugly, with a dark complexion, he had specialised in questioning suspects for many years and knew every possible and conceivable way of breaking down the resistance of those who fell into his hands. He had been at this type of work for so long that any spark of humanity in him had long ago vanished. Quite simply, Sergeant Amura was a cruel sadistic monster.

Amura's immediate superior, who I was to meet later, was Lieutenant Tanashi. He was a much younger man and a product of the up-and-coming officer class, ruthless and determined to make a name for himself in the Kempi Tai. While Sergeant Amura specialised in getting his results through inflicting physical pain, Tanashi used more subtle ways, believing that it was possible to achieve his ends by mentally breaking down the resistance of those he questioned. The Kempi Tai had long recognised that human beings could not stand intense pain, loneliness, hunger, bright lights, intermittent noise and other cruel mental and physical assaults now used by many nations.

Furthermore, the Kempi Tai were never in a hurry. The only important thing was to have the captive sign his own death warrant by finally confessing to whatever charges it suited them to bring against him. If they were short of work they would send out soldiers to round up any given group, put them through the grinder and come up with more impressive numbers of enemies of Japan.

Sergeant Amura stood looking at me, sizing me up to decide which system he would use first.

He had a young Japanese interpreter with him and another soldier who was to take down whatever Amura told him to write. The questions for a start were simple and caused no problem. As previously, they were about my family and where I lived. As they already had this information, there was no problem in repeating it. But once all this early stuff was complete, the real fun began. Sergeant Amura asked if I was a saboteur. Well I knew I was, but he wasn't going to, so I denied any such allegation. The first blow was struck — just an open hand across my face — and the question was repeated. The same answer brought a number of blows across my back with his sword, in its scabbard. This really hurt. When I again gave the same answer to the same question I was thrown against the wall, kicked in the stomach and groin, and then beaten across the legs with a lump of wood. I was now barely conscious, bleeding from the mouth, and there were a number of bad cuts on my legs. Finally, Amura kicked me in the head and I went out like a light.

I came to with Mac holding my head, trying to staunch the blood flowing from my nose. 'What are they onto now' he whispered. I told him that the new approach was that we were saboteurs, and that the bugger of a Jap NCO was a mad brutal animal. Play it simple and appear very frightened, I advised Mac. I had made the mistake of appearing stubborn and knew he would take delight in breaking me if he could. The Bishop, who was in bad shape himself, crawled over near me and quietly said a prayer for our salvation. That evening I managed to eat the rice ball and had some cold tea. I knew that I would have to try to get through tomorrow's interrogation without falling into any traps. Sure enough, I was one of those taken out first.

Upstairs I met Lieutenant Tanashi. At first glance he seemed to be a nice young man, which shows how looks can deceive. He sat and watched as Sergeant Amura started in on me. This time he changed the question to which guerilla fighters I knew or had met. Naturally I denied any knowledge of them. Amura promptly struck me across the head and mouth and repeated the question. When I repeated my answer, he knocked me to the floor, pushed me on my face, stood on my legs, grabbed both my wrists and started to bend me backwards. As the pressure got stronger I started to yell in pain but all he did was increase the pressure on my wrists. I passed out and was brought around by the soldier throwing a bucket of water over me. Then I was dragged to the chair in front of Lieutenant Tanashi's table and he quietly said, in reasonable English, that he would like to talk with me. He sent Amura out of the room but a soldier remained to take down any notes.

There was no need for all the pain and anguish I was suffering, Tanashi told me. The Kempi Tai already knew quite a lot about us, he said, but they needed our full story before they could decide what to do with us. It was up to me to convince the lieutenant that we were not spies and saboteurs.

There seemed nothing to gain by refusing to defend myself, so I simply gave him the cover story. Tanashi listened and then grew very angry, calling me a fool and saying that I must be a spy. My story was stupid and full of lies, he said. How could we exist for so long without help? Tanashi stood over me, red in the face, swore in Japanese and smacked me hard. He had lost his temper and as he stormed out of the room called Sergeant Amura, who came back smiling. He had no time for the soft approach and was happy to prove that his ways were the only ones that worked.

This time Amura sent out for buckets of water and a funnel. I was held down, the funnel was forced down my throat and they began pouring water into the funnel. In no time I was blown up like a balloon and when no more water could be forced down Amura started to beat my stomach with a rattan cane which split the skin and caused me agony in my insides. I was barely conscious, but they kicked me in the body which created intense pain. I was urinating and couldn't stop, water was flowing from my mouth and nose and I could hardly breathe. Finally I fell unconscious and was apparently dragged back to the pen where Mac and some of the others slowly revived me.

I didn't know how much more I could take,

and the Japanese were obviously playing a game with Mac, knowing that each time I came back he knew what he could expect. It was a kind of subtle torture before the event. I had difficulty in eating and it was agonisingly painful to urinate, which I was continually forced to do. Somehow I managed to get a few hours sleep, though it was hard to face the fact that I would be back in the torture chamber the next day. The Bishop, who was now being left alone, was a great comfort to us all. He was a wonderful man, whose presence in that hellhole helped many of us get through the terrible days of torture and degradation.

The next day, my treatment moved to a second phase. I was taken out of the pen and down the corridor to a single cell. It was a small windowless room that could almost be called a cupboard and was completely bare, with only a bucket. This was to be my home for the next few weeks. Mac would not know whether I was alive or dead and this was clearly another part of their approach to break us down, as neither of us would know what happened to the other. Complete isolation was another form of torture in this small locked room. I didn't know whether it was day or night, I had no watch, the light was on all the time, and a guard spied on me at will through a small panel in the door.

The only indication of time came when they gave me a ball of rice and a mug of warm tea. I tried speaking to the guard but his reply was a slap across the face, so I was left with my own thoughts and the hope that I could convince my captors that our story was true.

Next morning I was taken upstairs again. This time Sergeant Amura had some electric flex and what appeared to be a transformer, which he plugged into the power point before he started his interrogation. His questions were designed to make me admit that we had been with the guerilla forces, and he would not deviate from this theme all the time I was with him. After I denied we even knew such forces existed, he tied me to the chair, turned on the power and, taking the two bare ends of the electrical wires, he held them against either side of my left hand. I screamed with the pain and my body arched in the chair. When he repeated his question I tried to give him the same answer in a different way, but Amura would have none of it and repeated the treatment. Amura decided that this was not enough fun so he pulled my pants down and applied the wires to my testicles. The agony was unbearable and I screamed and passed out. I came to, back in my small cell.

Over the next week every day was a nightmare. Amura had me brought to him for interrogation each morning. I received water each day but the guard often tipped my food on the floor and walked on it in. Sometimes he tipped it over me. It was all part of a general harassment, to try and break my spirit. Each day Amura and I covered the same ground, though I was slowly letting out information to questions within the terms of the cover story Mac and I had agreed on. Through the interpreter Amura told me many times that Mac had already confessed to being a spy and a saboteur, but I knew this was a lie. Mac would never go outside our cover story. Day after day I was returned to the cell bleeding and unconscious, and I was sure the same was happening to Mac.

I had by now lost a number of fingernails and toenails, which Amura and his sadistic assistant pulled out with a pair of pliers. And a number of my fingers were infected where they had driven slivers of bamboo under the nails. There seemed little left that they hadn't tried. At the same time it was proving more difficult for them to continue the torture for any length of time as I was now blacking out on a very low threshold of pain. I was deteriorating in health very rapidly and knew I would not be able to stay on my feet much longer. The continual beatings, the water treatment which I had now had more than six times, plus the electric shocks and the other violations of my body were pushing my heart to the edge. I think even Amura realised that he had just about run out of time. He had not got any new information from me for several days and I was finding it hard to think clearly anyway. I think I was close to losing any hope of survival. Even through all this torture and degradation I thought, if I get through this I will learn to speak Japanese if it's the last thing I do. If I could understand what they were talking about it would go a long way to helping me survive. I had already picked up quite a few words that had been repeated to me since we had been betrayed to the Japanese.

Suddenly I was left strictly alone. The guards checked in on me throughout the day and nights and I was given water, twice as much food, and even some toilet paper — a luxury I hadn't enjoyed since we were recaptured. Something was happening. I tried to get the guards to talk to me. They were either too scared or keener to push me around, but they weren't beating me any more. There had to be a reason for this change of attitude, and although I didn't know what it was I welcomed the chance to recover from the results of my inquisition. Each day seemed to last an eternity, however, and I wondered if Mac was still there.

Then came the day that changed our lives for the next few years. I was called out of my cell and taken to a bathroom where the guard gave me a razor and told me to shave. Then I was to shower. My dirty clothes were thrown out and I was given freshly washed shorts, an army shirt and a pair of thongs. I was allowed to use a comb that was in the bathroom, and when I finally looked reasonably presentable I was taken into a small room and told to sit down on the floor.

The guard and I waited here for about half an hour before another guard brought Mac in. Mac had also had the clean-up treatment and it was great to see him and to know he was also still alive after the going-over we had both survived.

We were not allowed to talk to each other and had to remain seated on the floor until a young officer entered. No-one spoke English so we had no idea what was going to happen, but when they made us stand up and a rope was placed around our necks we feared the worst.

We were taken to a large office where a lieutenant collected some sheets of paper, all printed in Japanese, put them in front of us and told us to sign the bottom of each page. There was not much we could do other than sign, and having completed this we were taken out of the building into a waiting truck which took us through the streets of Singapore towards the waterfront. We drove in the back of a large building with a dome. It was the Supreme Court building and we were going to be tried.

THIRTEEN

Japanese court martial

Mac and I were taken into a small antechamber and told to sit. The rope was taken off and we were allowed to talk to each other. We had so much to ask each other that the time passed very quickly. It was obvious we had been cleaned up so the court wouldn't see how badly we had been treated, though they would have to be pretty silly not to notice the cuts, bruises and swellings which gave the game away.

Finally we were told to follow the guard into the main courtroom where five officers, the most senior was obviously a general, were seated on a carved bench. There was also a prosecutor, a Japanese captain, who had the papers we had signed and a wad of other reports, presumably from the Kempi Tai in Johore Bahru and Singapore. The General often asked the prosecutor questions but the whole trial only took about half an hour. Mac and I just stood in the dock. We were not spoken to at any stage, nor did we have any idea what was happening. Finally the General stood up. Everyone bowed to each other, our judges left the court and we were taken back to the anteroom. The guard looked at us and used his hands to indicate that our throats would be cut. Mac and I remained quiet. The fact that the guard was probably right had shut out any other thoughts for the time being.

However, another Guard came in a while later and he spoke enough English to tell us that we were very lucky. In consideration of our age the court had been very lenient he told us. We had been sentenced to two years solitary confinement in a Japanese Army gaol — the notorious Outram Road.

FOURTEEN

Outram Road Gaol

Two new guards with an officer came into the anteroom and we were formally handed over to the guards from Outram Road Gaol. The old guards waited while what must have been our release papers were completed, then immediately put handcuffs on us and a rope around our necks. That was the last time for two years that John 'Mac' McGregor and I were able to have any conversation without attracting the harshest punishment.

We were driven through the Singapore business centre to Outram Road Gaol. By the time we passed through the gates Mac and I had already drawn fire from the two guards when we tried to talk to each other. From now on this was strictly forbidden. We were taken to a small room, stripped of our clothes and issued with a Japanese army shirt and a pair of shorts then fingerprinted and photographed. All the while we were under strict surveillance and not allowed to open our mouths. An officer made it quite plain that our sentence had already commenced and that solitary confinement meant exactly what it implied. After processing we were taken to a large three-storey cell block and lodged in single cells on the ground floor. We were then pushed into cells, fortunately alongside each other, and the doors were slammed shut.

My cell was about ten feet long, and by stretching out both arms I could nearly touch each side. The ceiling was about fourteen feet high and there was a small barred window about two feet down from the ceiling. The door, which was thick and had an old-fashioned lock, had a small grille near its base, and a peephole at shoulder height, both of which could be opened from the outside. The only items in the cell were three bed boards, each about eight inches wide and seven feet long, a curved wooden pillow and a metal bucket for a toilet. This was to be my home for the next two years unless the war finished before then. The cell was filthy, the walls dirty and scratched with foreign writings, and only a little light came in through the high, small window with its four vertical iron bars and a thick mesh wire which was rusty and dirty. However, as I was to discover, the single light hanging from the ceiling was never turned off.

We had not been in our cells very long before the door opened and I had my first visitor — a Korean guard. He introduced himself by beating me across the back with a wooden baton, screaming at me in Korean, and somehow making me understand that I wasn't free to wander around the cell. Each time the bell was rung I was to sit on the floor for an hour facing the door in a special way. The position changed each hour at the sound of the bell being rung. The first position was kneeling on the floor, then sitting back on my legs. When the bell rang again I was to change the position to sitting with my legs crossed with my left arm across between my knees and the right arm vertical and the elbow on my right thigh. Both these punishment positions were extremely uncomfortable.

It didn't take me long to catch on as the guard came in and beat me with his baton until I was obeying the rules. From the sounds next door Mac was also being brought into line. However, as the outside floor was concrete we soon learnt to hear the guards as they approached our cells. As time passed our hearing became more acute. We could hear the creak of the guards equipment as they approached, and quickly learnt how to adjust our position to take the pressure off our muscles. We would fall into these rest positions once the guard had passed by, checking on each cell.

Probably the, most difficult thing to face was the almost complete silence. After the weeks we had spent in the Kempi Tai interrogation centre, the gaol was like a tomb. Pretty well the only sounds we heard were made by the guards' equipment and boots. Occasionally the drone of a plane flying high above would filter in through the window. It is amazing how quickly solitude can eat into your soul when it is enforced and there is nothing you can do about it. Solitary confinement would quickly destroy anyone who was weak-willed, or didn't have a good reason to fight back, or loved ones to whom he was determined to return.

Before long Mac and I started to tap morse code messages to each other through the wall. As time passed we found we could quickly — with abbreviations and shortened sentences — carry on a reasonable discussion. In those early days this kept us both from going mad.

However, we wouldn't dare signal to each other or move from our appointed position when certain guards were on duty. They wore rubber-soled split-toed boots that made no sound on the concrete. The only warning you had was if your ears were good enough to pick up the creak of their equipment, or perhaps the sound of their scabbard hitting their legs.

Before the war the British had used Outram Road gaol for Indian and Chinese offenders. It was a massive old building surrounded by a high brick wall and barbed wire with a number of sentry towers. The grounds and courtyards were in good condition but the Japanese had purposely let the cells remain dirty, full of bugs and lice, as part of the prisoners' punishment. The corridors and their own quarters were kept in perfect condition, and when inspections were made by outside officials the steps up to the cells were scrubbed clean.

At first the food at Outram Road was the best we had enjoyed since being recaptured. We received a small bun with a cup of soup in the morning, a small ball of rice and sometimes a couple of part dried-plums late in the afternoon, along with more rice, a few green vegetables and some green tea. While the diet was barely enough to survive on, we did not contract beri-beri and our weight appeared to remain stable. However, it was not long before the Japanese decided that we would not receive the same rations as their own army prisoners on the second and third floors. Later as the war turned against them, the rations were further reduced. There were more than 1200 deaths at Outram Road in the two years of our incarceration, and some of these were Japanese prisoners. By the end of the ninth month our rations had been so reduced that we were all steadily losing weight. My normal weight before capture was 11 stone but when I was released back to Changi I weighed 6 stone 4½ pounds, Mac, who normally weighed 13 stone, was just under 7 stone.

I had lost all sense of time since my recapture but I managed to find out the date from a guard when we were going to the prison. I scratched it on the wall of my cell so that we would at least know the day and month. Simple things like this became essential to our determination to survive. You could visualise what your loved ones were doing on a given day. This was an essential part of refusing to let the Japanese destroy your will to survive.

The first week in Outram Road was a nightmare. With only a rudimentary idea of Japanese culture and behaviour, we had moved into another world where most of what we had learnt beforehand was of no use to us. We had to adjust quickly to life in a Japanese penal situation as those who learnt the fastest would have the best chances of survival. The day after we arrived I managed to tap out in morse to Mac that I was going to try to learn Japanese in a hurry. His answer was 'Go ... Go' as he also appreciated that we were going to need to use our wits if we were to get out of here alive.

I had worked out my options. I could refuse to cooperate with the gaol authorities and be as difficult as possible, or I could cooperate only as much as would be necessary to survive. A third option was to cooperate and learn Japanese as quickly as possible. Not only would I then know what was going on, but I would be able to present appeals for any urgent needs that arose. And I felt sure that speaking to the Japanese in their own language, would ensure that they would at least listen to me. Learning their difficult language also gave me a useful occupation to help pass the time.

The choice was simple and I started to learn Japanese on the third day we entered Outram Road. I reckoned the only way to go would be to get the guards to give me the Japanese names for fifteen objects a day and for me to learn them by heart. This was no mean feat, seeing I had no paper or books or pencils to assist me. Even though we were not permitted to talk, the guards were intrigued at my wanting to learn their language, which they referred to as Nippon-Go. I started with the body, and by using what I learnt with the next guard on duty I was able to check each word and its pronunciation. It was the beginning of a long and difficult process, but as time progressed the guards started to look on me as their own personal project. There were several guards I made no attempt to speak to, but it was not long before even they spoke to me. Other guards must have told them what I was about. As time went on I think several of them almost entered into competition to take me over. However, don't be deceived by this interest, it was only there when it suited the individual, and many of them would still beat me up for the smallest infringement. None of us got used to the wide personality swings that any one guard could exhibit in a matter of moments.

Mac and I contacted each other through the wall, using morse code. At first, a simple sentence took a considerable time to transmit, but we developed abbreviations. It helped pass many hours each day for us. I don't think anyone has any conception of the stages that your brain passes through when you are suddenly left on your own, in a confined space, with the realisation that you have years ahead of you in this debilitating situation. In my period at Outram Road I heard every reaction. Some inmates screamed until they were silenced by a guard. Others never stopped. They went just mad and screamed and beat their heads on the walls. Those who went mad inevitably died as the Japanese response to such behaviour was to withhold food and take out the bed boards and pillow and toilet bucket. From then on these prisoners roamed the cell as long as they could walk, and often finished up beating themselves to death on the walls of the cell. It was only then that the cell was opened and the body carted out for disposal. Absolutely no attempt was made to treat them medically. The same was true for inmates suffering from beri-beri and dysentery. All food would be withdrawn from them and few recovered sufficiently to be fed again. This was a savage jungle environment in which the guards and their officers were the predators. If you showed any signs of weakness you were virtually written off.

I continued to learn at least fifteen words of Japanese a day and somehow managed to keep reasonably sane in those first few weeks.

At 6 a.m. each day a bell rang loudly and the guard ran around screaming at the inmates to get up. Then he started opening doors for four persons at a time to take out their toilet bucket for emptying into a disposal tank in the courtyard. Two other guards were also on duty, making sure no prisoners got close to each other or made any attempt to talk. We were marched out quickly, amid screaming commands from all three, to empty the bucket and rinse it out with some water in a trough, making sure we didn't spill the contents on ourselves as we were not permitted to wash, and marched back into our cells. Then another four were taken out. At 7 a.m our breakfast was put through the door. About half an hour later the plate and mug were taken away and our day of punishment commenced. The bell rang at 8 a.m. And the first position of kneeling was adopted. An hour later the bell rang again and we changed to position two. This went on until 5 p.m, when we were given our other meal for the day. This was the pattern of our lives for the two years.

In those first weeks the numbers in the gaol increased, and a few more English and Australian soldiers were among the new inmates. Two of them were put in cells alongside Mac and two English officers were put in cells beside mine. We were soon quickly tapping on our walls to see if they would respond. The prisoner in the cell next to mine knew morse code so we were soon able to trade information. In the meantime Mac contacted the inmate who was next to him, and we soon established a line of communication through six cells. This kept us busy for a long time as we had to move from wall to wall to send signals to each other in between the rounds of the guards, who sensed that something was going on and tried creeping up on our cells. Luckily for us, their equipment usually gave them away and we warned each other as we heard them approach. It was a risky business, and if any of us were caught out the guard would open the door and beat the hell out of the culprit, leaving him only after he was bleeding profusely. Despite the risks involved, we were able to carry out this form of contact for about six months. When the guards finally worked out what was happening they moved everyone around so that each of us had an Asian prisoner in between. All contact was lost.

The sergeant major, who was aged about forty and was known as the Cat for some reason, was a daily visitor. He had a large drooping moustache, wore glasses and was tall for a Jap — about 5 feet 10 or 11. From his behaviour I would say he was well educated and came from a good family. Although he was a strict disciplinarian, I learnt to respect him in the two years I was there. Within the limits of his authority, he tried to maintain some sort of humane treatment of the prisoners and to defuse the sadism of his commanding officer. There were two Korean sergeants, one of whom was a very easygoing, lazy, fat and simple soul, the other determined to prove to his Japanese masters that he could do the job as cruelly as they could. Under these two sergeants there were about forty or fifty Japanese and Korean soldiers, two of whom I discovered had been educated in England. They spoke English well but didn't want anyone else to know, as they would get a hard time from their colleagues.

Amongst the rest there were five or six quite reasonable types who treated us decently when they were on their own but behaved just as badly as the others whenever anyone else was present. We came to realise their freedom was always on the line also. I quietly made an assessment of each guards' personality. If I was to learn Japanese, I had better work on the ones with whom I had the best prospects of getting cooperation. The best time for learning was always late at night, when everyone was asleep and the gaol was quiet. The friendlier guards could then afford to lean in the recess of my door and talk to me without much chance of being caught by their superiors.

Finally I had five guards teaching me Japanese when they came on duty at night. They started by giving me the names of various items I pointed to, and as I sat the next day I repeated them over and over, hour by hour, until they were stamped on my brain. It was a slow and laborious process but when I finally left the gaol I knew more Japanese words than English. After building a vocabulary, I gradually learnt verbs and adjectives and so on, until I could string sentences together — very badly at first, much to the amusement of my teachers. However, by the latter stages of my incarceration I was quite fluent. This early hard work saved my life more than once and helped many others. Eventually, the Cat discovered that I was becoming proficient in Japanese but he took no action to find out who had taught me. In fact when the sergeant major realised I could speak Nippon-Go I was often taken out of my cell and used as an interpreter when other Europeans were brought into the gaol. While Outram Road was essentially a Japanese military prison, primarily established to punish their own offenders, it was forced to take in increasing numbers of other races and nationalities.

The Japanese had a number of senior officers serving sentences for a variety of offences, the most common of which was failure to achieve a given objective in battle. Some of them were serving terms of up to twenty years and I gathered that few of them were sentenced to less than five years ... and these were for offences for which the Australian Army would dock two days pay or confine you to barracks for a while. It is no wonder, then, that the Japanese Army demanded and got such exacting obedience.

The day to day routine and conditions didn't change much for the first three months. However a steady intake of new prisoners led to a corresponding increase in the guards' strength. There appeared to be a number of European civilians confined, many of them in what I could see were in very poor physical condition. I made this discovery when I was taken out of my cell to move some timber that was being used to repair part of the cell block. I found myself outside a cell in which three Frenchmen were confined, and while the guard was busy some distance away I had a quick conversation with them. Their leader told me he was Count Francois de Corselles, the director of the French Indo-China Bank of Saigon. He and his two companions had been taken by the Japanese in retribution after it was discovered that the bank's reserves had been spirited out of

Indo-China just as the Japanese were entering.

We were only able to whisper for a few minutes, but I gave him my name and rank and told him where I came from. The count said he and his two friends intended to escape at the first chance and that he'd try to get my information back to Australian authorities. At that point the guard noticed that I was talking to them and stormed back, screaming at me to stop and move away.

I never saw Count de Corselles again. After the war I learned that he and his two companions were taken back to Indo-China for further questioning. They escaped, and after a long and difficult trek eventually found their way to Kunming, in China. True to his promise, the Count sent information about my whereabouts to Army headquarters in Australia. In Perth, my wife Bunny was amazed when she was summoned to Government house and told by the governor himself that they had received information through diplomatic channels that I was alive and well. Up until this time all she knew was that I was posted as missing, presumed to be a POW. It was still some months before the Red Cross released a list of Australian POWs in Singapore and Bunny was asked not to let anyone else know about this conversation. Apparently it was hoped that I had been able to establish some way of getting information out and they did not wish to compromise my position. I wrote to Count de Corselles after the war, care of the Indo-China Bank but, I never discovered if the letter reached him.

At one stage there was a large influx of civilian prisoners and a young Indian named Marjeet, who had been caught stealing from the Japanese stores, was put in to share my cell. He was a fascinating rogue who I am sure could steal the shirt off your back without you noticing. Marjeet was born in Calcutta and boasted that he had only survived to adulthood by being smart enough to suckle from his married sister, and he told me many fantastic tales of how the urchins created diversions in the marketplace to enable older members of their gangs to steal food. If only half of what he told me was true, he had lived a most extraordinary life and there appeared to be little he hadn't been involved in other than murder. The few weeks he spent with me passed quickly and I was sorry when they moved him to a cell on his own.

Things must have been going badly for the Japanese, as not only was the food ration cut severely, but the guards' tempers became worse. Inmates were dying daily and it was ghastly to hear the screaming of those in their death throes. The most fiendish guards took delight in taking the Europeans in to clean the cell after someone had died. It was a nauseating job, particularly if the inmate had been mentally disturbed and confined to his cell for weeks without any sanitary arrangements. Their excrement was all over the floor and even the walls, and in most cases there were also pools of blood and gore. It took hours to clean the cell with the few materials that were made available.

By this time I was making quite good progress with my Japanese and was occasionally pulled out of my cell to act as an interpreter. This gave me an opportunity to know who else was in the gaol and to find out as much as I could about them. I committed as much as I could to memory hoping it would be of later use, if any of us survived. Some of the older men who were brought in were in dreadful condition. One in particular I remember had been the chief engineer of the Singapore Board of Works. He was in his late fifties and when I first saw him he was grossly bloated from beri-beri. His legs were two or three times their normal size, his body was grotesque, and most of his facial features had disappeared within the flabby watery swelling that accompanies beri-beri. He was in dreadful agony but lasted four weeks without medical assistance before he died a terrible death. I doubt if he had been given any food. On several occasions I asked the few guards who were more likely to listen to me to help him, but I was always given the same answer. No-one who was confined to Outram Road would receive medical attention. This was considered part of the punishment ... if you lived, you lived, and if you died too bad.

Early in August of that first year I was taken out of my cell to a distant part of the gaol, where an Australian sergeant, E. S. Hatfield, was located. I was told by the guard that he was awaiting execution for an attempted escape. He had asked for a priest to hear his confession but his request had been denied. He was, however, allowed to see me and pass on a request. In the quarter of an hour they let me stay with him, Hatfield told me a good deal of his life and how anxious he was to make a will so his de facto wife in New Zealand could get his deferred pay and anything else he may be entitled to. I promised him that I would swear out an affidavit to this effect if I got home but I could do little else to help him. I felt utterly useless, but I think it gave him some comfort to know that a fellow Australian knew exactly what happened to him. In Singapore soon after the war I did as I had promised and I understand that his de facto wife received all due entitlements.

I spent a most unhappy time praying for Hatfield, and hoping that some day the Japanese responsible would pay for the crime they committed against this young man who did what all good soldiers are expected to do. The barbaric beheading they carried out indicates the warped mentality that we were dealing with. Sergeant Hatfield will live always in my memory as a brave young man who died bravely on his own.

It was becoming increasingly difficult to keep track of time. Each day was a repeat of the one before, and living in this semi-gloom with only distant and hard to decipher noises, other than the screams of prisoners in agony, it was only the thought of those we loved that kept us from also going down the path of madness and death.

The Japanese had been using an Indian and a Eurasian inmate to distribute the meals in our part of the gaol and they often ran out of food before they reached more than eighty per cent of the prisoners. They were clearly giving their friends extra helpings and I complained many times to the guards, especially those who were teaching me Japanese. When the matter finally reached the Cat he ordered me to supervise the distribution in future. When the food arrived from the kitchen, four buckets of rice and buckets of weak tea, I had all the dishes placed on a table and served there, to ensure that every plate had exactly the same amount. Still not trusting the two servers, I had the order of distribution changed for each meal so they had no way of regularly getting more to any one person. Naturally, those who had been getting larger servings immediately complained. The guards knew that these people had been receiving special attention so they went into their cells and gave them a good slap in the face.

That should have been the end of the matter, but two Australian officers tried to use rank and pressure on me to see that they were given extra food. I told them both what I thought of them and was told in response that I would regret not helping them. They both wrote complaints about me when they were released, but I gather they were themselves reprimanded when a check was made with other inmates of the gaol. I could have laid a complaint against them myself, but I was not interested in adding to the problems of conscience they would have to live with. I am pleased to say that the system I devised was used to distribute the meals, such as they were, for the rest of my captivity. Once it was working efficiently, the guards supervised the two servers.

To add to my woes, I was having great trouble with my teeth. I had dropped my two dentures as my loss of weight had made them very loose, and when the top plate dropped on the concrete a number of the false teeth had broken. Somehow I would have to repair the damage, but to do this I needed something to make new teeth from, and some wire to hold them in place. I also had to solve the problem of making holes through the plate for the wire. Everything connected with this enterprise would be difficult, as the Japanese had a phobia about prisoners having access to anything sharp or anything like wire.

I decided first of all to handle the problem of how to make the teeth. All I needed was a toothbrush handle. I hadn't seen one for a long time, of course, but the guards would have them. As for the wire, I suddenly realised it was staring me in the face. The mesh over the window was broken and there was plenty of wire up there. All I had to do was solve the small problem of getting about twelve feet up the wall. I spent hours thinking about it and eventually I worked out that the three bed boards could be used to create a type of zig-zag ladder. If I placed the end of one on the floor on one side of the cell, then the other end would be about three feet up the wall. The next board could be placed in reverse, giving me another three feet, and the third plank would be high enough to allow me to reach the wire over the window. It sounded great in theory, but if any of the guards saw me doing this they would immediately assume I was trying to escape and all hell would break loose. It would be nigh on impossible to convince them what I was really doing. This presented me with a new problem to solve, so I put the idea on hold and returned to the question of the toothbrush.

By now I had established pretty much exactly the character of each guard. There were only two who I could trust with anything that was not in the rule book. Both of them were Christians, though they would vigorously deny it to anyone else, and one had been educated outside Japan for part of his life. They were my best bet but I still needed to have a good story as to why I needed a toothbrush. When one of the guards I could trust came on duty I asked him if he had an old toothbrush I could have as I was experiencing trouble with my stomach because of germs on my teeth. I didn't think he believed me, but the next time he was on night duty he handed me a toothbrush. It had the old ivory-type handle and was just what I needed. I couldn't wait to get to work on making new teeth.

The next night a lazy guard I called Dopey

who usually slept through his shift in a doorway, came on late duty. Once he had settled down I set up my planks against the wall and as quietly as I could I climbed up and unthreaded some pieces of wire from the mesh. It all went without a hitch. I made some noise getting the bed planks down again but Dopey slept on and I don't think anyone knew what I had been up to.

Now the only problem I hadn't solved was how to bore holes through the plate itself. Well, Rome wasn't built in a day and time was not my problem — I had plenty of it with more than a year to go before I might leave here on my own two feet. Still, boring holes in a dental plate was a pretty tough assignment in Outram Road, and it seemed this one might beat me unless I could get access to something like a nail. This was something I could not request from even the most cooperative of guards, so I was on my own.

A gaol cell is not a good place to find nails and my only hope lay in the thick wooden cell door. I examined it thoroughly but there seemed to be only metal bolts used in its construction. However, a careful check of the grille at the foot of the door showed that one of the metal pieces had become a bit loose. If I could help it along and work it off the frame, I could then sharpen it on the concrete floor. It took me two weeks of patient work, night after night, but at last I had three inches of round thick wire ready for sharpening. I just had to hope that no-one would notice any change and conduct a search of my cell.

In fact this was a whole new problem I had to cope with, as the toothbrush, the wire from the window and now this three inch piece of thick wire all had to be hidden. Because the building was so old, there were many cracks in the walls and some gaps between the wall and the floors. So I scratched out the worst of one of these down at floor level, carefully keeping the dirt and debris, and was able to fit all my treasures in the space after I had broken the toothbrush in two. I then filled up the front with the dirt I had kept for this purpose. Unless one of the guards checked the whole floor with something sharp, he had little chance of finding my loot.

From now on I was a very busy boy. In between listening for the guards on their rounds, I steadily ground the toothbrush handle into teeth. It took weeks of careful work to produce the replacements but they looked the part and I was proud of my handwork. The next job was to make the tool up to bore holes through the plate, and I was immediately confronted with a fresh problem. The toothbrush handle I rubbed on the concrete floor didn't make much noise, but the metal I was to use for a punch was another matter and I could only sharpen it when there was some other loud noise in the building. At six each morning groups of inmates were taken out to empty their toilet buckets, and the guards were all busy, so I used the limited time between emptying my bucket and the guards taking the last group out. By the time I had finished and was ready to make the holes in the plate, I had been on this job alone for over two months. But the end was now in sight.

Eventually, all the necessary holes were bored and the indentations for each tooth had been gouged out. The wire I had taken down from the window was copper and easy to work with and when I finally had the teeth in place I wired each one in position. I had to find a way of ensuring that the ends of the wire were also hidden in the plate so they didn't irritate my gums. After a few final adjustments the plate was ready to use again.

When I returned to Changi the doctors were amazed at how well I had replicated the original teeth. And not a single Jap knew what was being done before his eyes. I used the plate for the remainder of my time as a POW and it was not replaced until I returned to Australia.

FIFTEEN

The second year

The first year had slipped away and, early one morning in June 1943, I heard Australian voices — obviously a working party — in the courtyard outside my cell block. It was great to hear those voices, and their swearing. 'Fancy making us work here with all those Nip bastards inside.' I was tempted to call out to them, but this would only bring the guard down on me and there was little chance that the POWs outside would hear me, even though I could hear what they were saying to each other very clearly. Two of them were talking just under my window and one said, 'I think this is where that bloke Dean is. Maybe we can get a message to him.' I couldn't hear the rest of what they were saying, but I gathered they were waiting for the guard to get further away or become preoccupied with something else.

While I was wondering how they would do this, a piece of paper wrapped around a stone came hurtling through my window. I heard the guard scream at them. He must have suspected they were up to something, but didn't know what.

Scrawled on the paper was 'Tell Deany he has a son'. That was all. For the first time I learned that my son Michael had been born. I hadn't even known that Bunny was pregnant. This was a most remarkable occurrence. Out of all the cells along that wall they had thrown the message direct to me. It was most unlikely that I would have got it had it gone into any of the other cells.

When I finally got back to Changi I spent weeks trying to find out who had thrown the message in, so I could thank him for the boost it gave me, but I never discovered who it was. The most I could learn was that POWs working in Borneo had received cards from home via the Vatican, and one of these mentioned that I had a son. Some of those POWs were transferred to Singapore to go to Thailand to work on the railway, and they must have left the information with someone in Changi. That someone was kind enough to get the message to me in Outram Road.

This incident was a particularly strong factor in my determination to survive my term in gaol. I knew the second year would be worse than the first, as the rations had been cut even further and many of the guards had been replaced with those not reckoned to be fit for active service. The Japanese were losing ground and the new lot of guards were a bunch of sadistic animals.

My Japanese had reached a stage where I had become fluent enough to pick up information from the guards' conversation. And even they were now aware that they were no longer having easy victories, and they often spoke about withdrawals to new positions. Almost daily I was being taken out to act as interpreter with new arrivals; the

Japanese were tightening their control on POWs, anyone caught trading with them and, in a few cases, escapees.

By the time they reached Outram Road these prisoners were in pretty bad shape, most having spent a month or so with the Kempi Tai. They were resigned to their fate and were glad of any help I could give them. Usually, all I could do was warn them how to keep out of trouble. However, there were some very difficult and troublesome prisoners and, sadly, I have to admit they included Australian officers. Because of their stupidity and ignorance, they were on a number of occasions responsible for all of us having our rations withdrawn for several days at a time. The two I already had to put up with were quickly joined by two others who were even more stupid. The remaining forty-odd Australian and English soldiers quickly woke up to them and gave them short shrift when these officers tried to stand over them.

Meanwhile, I had been steadily working on the two guards who had spent time teaching me Japanese. They were way ahead of the others and were quite humane under the front they put on for their fellow guards and their superiors. I knew that whatever chance there was of us getting out of here alive depended on somehow getting our hands on some vitamin B tablets. The guards were taking them to counter beri-beri and, somehow, I had to persuade them to supply us also. The only weapon I had going for me was their knowledge that the war wasn't going their way and that it might be advantageous to have friends on their side. We were all showing signs of beri-beri and our days were numbered if we couldn't get some help.

I talked for hours with these two guards when they were on the late night shift. They were not hard to get on with and they appreciated our need for vitamin B. Their main worry was that while it would be easy to get some for me, they would themselves become long-term prisoners if they were caught. But self-protection works both ways and they were very much aware of the possibility of the Japanese losing the war. I must admit I laid on the promises of the help I could give them. I knew I had no hope of fulfilling all I promised, but the circumstances left no room to be to choosy with the truth. Finally, one of my friends came on late duty and presented me with about fifty tablets. He dared not leave the bottle in case of a snap search but he told me that there was a large supply in the store, which had been captured on the fall of Singapore.

At this time there were seventeen Australian and English troops in the cells near me. The remainder were too far away for me to consider helping, but I had three tablets for each of those I hoped to supply. However, the problem of how to distribute them was another matter. The guard had only meant for me to take them and it took me a while longer to make him see that the more of us he could claim to have helped, then the more help he could expect in return. He finally bought the idea but there was a catch. He did not have access to keys at night so the tablets could only be distributed on the morning trip out with our toilet buckets. It took nearly a week to get them to the right people, but this was enough to halt the downhill slide into beri-beri. It was, however, only temporary relief and we needed to get tablets reasonably regularly. In one way this worked to our advantage, as we could not afford to suddenly appear to be recovering from beri-beri all at the same time.

Accidentally, I had learnt how I could get out of my cell at any time I desired. This was an old building with the old-fashioned system of a single lock on each door with a universal key. All I had to do was to place a piece of material in the lock slot before the door shut and a gentle pressure would push the lock back enough to open the door. I had worked this out when exploring the possibility of escape, but the main obstacle was the door out of the block, plus the other inmates who would soon arouse a guard anyway, so the only escape route was through the window. I already knew how to get up to that, but removing two bars would be a long and difficult exercise. Better to use my brains and my knowledge of the Japanese language to see out my time, using every trick I could to survive, and to help Mac do the same.

By this time Mac was about six cells away from me. I could only see him when we were emptying our toilet buckets, but I knew the vitamin B tablets and the promise of more to come helped his morale and his health. Also, Mac was a fitness fanatic and was able to keep his body going. His main problem was his eyesight, which was deteriorating fast. Hopefully the vitamin B would slow this process down.

At least once a week for the next four months, my guard friend gave me further tablets. As far as I know the Japanese officers in the gaol never knew that their stocks of vitamin B were being supplied to us, but there is no doubt the cooperative guards saved a lot of lives. After the war I made a report on this, as well as other reports on the brutal guards and officers, but I doubt that the helpful ones were ever recognised. Both these guards had been sent to the front a long time before the war ended.

As well as providing us with the vitamin B tablets, and having committed themselves to helping us, these two guards often brought small sweet cakes in with them at night, which they distributed amongst the Australian and English inmates. Who knows just how much this contributed to the survival of those they helped, and at such a great risk?

We were all suffering from problems caused by the inadequate food. I had developed a lump on my buttock which became infected and grew until it was nearly as large as a football. It was extremely painful but, try as I could, I couldn't get any of the guards to do anything about it until one day when the Cat inspected the cells on a snap search. He was amazed to see what had happened to me and it was the first time I ever saw him show any anger. He screamed at the guard to bring me out of the cell. I thought I was going to be taken to the dispensary but I was made to lie down alongside a gutter in the courtyard. My pants were then pulled down, exposing this great bloated lump, and I watched in horror when the Cat took out his sword. The next thing I knew he sliced the top off the lump and the blood and pus poured into the gutter. The relief that followed was beyond comprehension. Having done his bit of surgery, the Cat marched off, leaving me to the guards who thought the whole thing a great joke. They provided no water or assistance, but in his way the Cat had done me a great favour.

As I lay there with the guards laughing their heads off, it didn't take the blowflies long to find me and they had blown the whole horrible mess within minutes. When I tried to brush them off, the guards screamed at me to leave them be, and for once they knew what they were talking about. They explained to me the quickest way to heal such a wound was to let the maggots eat away all the bad flesh. It sounds barbaric but it worked. For the next week I lay in my cell with my buttocks crawling with maggots. The guards kept checking to see that my wound was healing, and within the fortnight it had cleared up. I was left, however, with a large scar to remind me of my courtyard surgery.

Mac's condition had deteriorated and he was at a very low ebb. His eyesight was going downhill fast and I pushed all I could to get medical attention for him, even taking the risk of speaking directly to the Cat on one of his visits. He listened to me without comment. I believe that there must have been other reasons for the move, but Mac was transferred to Changi's hospital, where he was put in isolation from the other sick and not allowed to have outside contact. In other words, he was still in solitary. However, this was ignored by our doctors and he was allowed visitors, without the Japs ever finding out. I heard when I finally got back to Changi that there had been some Swiss representatives from the Red Cross in Singapore at the time, and perhaps the Japanese didn't want any more POW deaths in Outram Road. At any rate, Mac was out, at least for the time being. In fact our doctors saw to it that he never returned to Outram Road. He was repatriated to Australia after the war, but permanently incapacitated.

In the early part of my second year, the numbers arriving in Outram Road rapidly increased, and this may have helped in our efforts to get four more Australians who were in the final stages of beri-beri, out to Changi to join Mac. Many of the cells had two Chinese or Indian prisoners, food was extremely short and the guards were becoming particularly brutal. The death rate was increasing alarmingly, and it was about this time that the two guards with whom I had been able to establish a good rapport were transferred. I had great difficulty in reaching any of the new ones, who all seemed scared to death of the senior NCOs and officers.

March came and went and I had only a few weeks to complete my sentence. Over that time I had grown accustomed to the daily routine. I was still beaten by the guards whenever they caught me off-guard, daydreaming, my mind away in Australia with my wife and children, but I had learnt how to avoid the worst of the blows and how to distract the guards' attention by asking them about their families. This usually made them stop. They were simple souls, without much on top, and strangely hungry for someone to treat them like human beings. April really dragged, each day seemed an eternity, and I almost counted the hours that were bringing me to May, when I was supposed to be released. To the best of my knowledge, no-one had ever left here alive, unless they were very sick, and I was hoping to be the first. I kept wondering if the Japs would find some excuse to keep me here.

On a Monday, two years to the day after I had been sentenced, a guard came and opened my door and said I was to return to Changi. I tried to speak to some of the other prisoners but the guards hurried me out to the office, made me change into my own clothes and put me in a truck. Then I was off. I was signed for by a Changi guard and put in the top of the tower at the gaol entrance.

SIXTEEN

Return to Changi

While I had been in Outram Road, the POWs had been moved from the Selerang Barracks to Changi gaol and the civilian internees relocated. I found myself once again locked in a room alone. It was also pretty bare, but this time I had an Indian bed to sleep on. At midday the Japanese guard who had been stationed outside the room brought me in a plate of rice and vegetables with a mug of tea. When I asked him what was going on he told me that Lieutenant Tagahashi would be coming to see me.

At about four o'clock Tagahashi and another Jap soldier came in. The lieutenant addressed me in Japanese and told me that, before I could be released into the camp, I was to sign a form saying that I would not attempt any escape, and that I understood I would be executed once I was caught if I did. He did not seem surprised when I told him I wasn't prepared to sign any such undertaking and just asked me to think about it. I would remain locked in my room until I signed.

Several times I had the guard take me to a toilet on the level below, and each time care was taken to see that no-one was anywhere nearby. Once again I was in solitary. Tuesday came and went. I could hear the sounds of a busy camp below my lofty prison, but no-one seemed to be doing anything to get me out. Little did I know that the whole camp knew I was there, and knew that the Japs wouldn't release me until I signed the non-escape form. Finally on Wednesday afternoon Tagahashi appeared and told me he had arranged for Lieutenant Colonel 'Black Jack' Galleghan to come and talk to me. Black Jack appeared later and told me not to worry about signing the form. Everyone else had and Black Jack told me it didn't count if it was signed under duress. His main priority was to get me into hospital, where the doctors could check me over. He already knew something of what I had been through and told me I wouldn't be expected to do anything again until we were released. 'And that's a promise' he added.

After Black Jack had left I told the guard I was ready to complete the required form, which I did there and then. Within the hour Tagahashi had released me to the hospital, where I was immediately given an examination to see what special treatment, if any, was needed. Dr Glynn White was very kind to me, quietly checking my heart and blood pressure and gradually getting information. The orderlies, other patients and all the doctors did everything they could to make me feel that I was back among friends, and the week I spent in the hospital helped make up for the bad days of the past two years. I spent every spare moment seeing Mac, who had made great progress, but great care had to be taken to see that the Japs didn't discover how well he was going or they would have sent him back to Outram Road to complete his sentence.

I had many visitors, some of whom were total strangers enquiring about some of the others imprisoned in Outram Road. And I had to spend some time at Lieutenant Colonel Galleghan's headquarters detailing all I knew about conditions in Outram Road, which prisoners were there, and their chances of getting out alive. I made a detailed report which included the problems I had faced with several Australian officers who had tried to pull rank on me to get special treatment. The major taking the report was not very pleased with this information, especially as it involved a field officer and an airforce officer. Still, it was a good thing that I put this in my report, as when two of these officers were finally released they filed an adverse report on my treatment of them. Later, a number of the English officers in Outram Road took the trouble to write to Australian Army HQ, advising them how I had been able to assist them, especially with the vitamin B tablets.

While I was making my report, Black Jack told me that he had arranged for me to share a room with Captain George Gwynne, a Company Commander in my battalion, so I could gradually resume my place in the life of the camp. George picked me up at the hospital and we made our way to the room at the end of one of the long attap huts in the officers' lines outside the main gaol building. There seemed to be a rumour circulating that I had gone balmy during my incarceration and some people treated me as though I was now a bit slow. I found this highly amusing and George and I had many laughs behind their backs.

Mind you, I don't think I was exactly normal. I found crowds difficult to deal with and Changi was a world I knew nothing about — it had developed while I was out of circulation. There were many troublesome people there, including a complete society of hustlers and black-marketeers. Thieving was rife and, sadly, hospital drugs and equipment were the prime targets of a highly organised gang operating many rackets.

This was a new experience. There were sixty men to a hut — a mixture of personalities that would not be encountered in such a confined area in any normal circumstances. For instance, in the hut I was now living in we had a lieutenant named Tony who bred rats for food. He had two cages and kept a close watch on them to see that no-one pinched his rodents. Another captain had a locked metal trunk which he never opened when anyone could see inside. Then there were the four who played contract bridge day after day, with some of them thousands of pounds in debt. We also had several yoga freaks, a number of whom hardly ever spoke, and a few who were already well around the bend. The worst one we had in the hut was the guy who had not taken a bath in years, and who had a matted beard and wild eyes.

This was a world of fantasy to me. There were some weirdos in Outram Road but some of those blokes in Changi would have put them to shame. George explained that the lack of an organised daily routine, and of something to work for, had led to many of the officers losing heart and drifting into strange habits.

I took the opportunity to examine the whole camp area. The gaol building to which the general troops had been assigned had been built to house about 500 prisoners but it now held many thousands. Outside the gaol wall were a number of large attap huts surrounded by a barbed-wire fence. A group of these huts had been assigned to the POW officers, while the houses that had been built for the gaol staff were now occupied by the Japanese camp staff and commander. Each day a large number of POWs were marched out of the camp to work on the new airfield being built nearby.

These first two years had taken their toll physically and the POWs showed deterioration, with many signs of malnutrition. The hospital was always full and though a large area had been set aside for vegetable gardens it could not provide the huge amounts required to maintain the Changi population. Hunger was everyone's companion, and most of the daylight hours were spent in chasing elusive sources of extra food.

Those who were best fed were the crooks who were in nightly contact with Chinese traders. They would sell goods inside for about five times as much as they had paid for them. Drugs in particular were worth very large amounts. Then these vultures made the local currency available to anyone silly enough to buy it at inflated prices, redeemable after the war.

When things got very bad I bought into this racket and got enough money to buy a pound of shelled peanuts, at a huge cost, which I owed to a lieutenant from northern New South Wales. Within weeks of getting home he wrote to remind me of the debt. How deeply he was involved with the racket I am not sure but I know of a number of others who owed him large sums also.

The hospital had to guard their limited amount of drugs against those constantly seeking something saleable and the standard of living maintained by some of the officers would make one believe that they were somehow involved. I was especially suspicious of those who appeared to have a good supply of clean clothes and had men who did a number of jobs for them — washing and pressing clothes and repairing and cleaning their boots, of which they had more than one pair.

The shortage of food, the constant thieving and the inevitable misunderstandings between nationalities caused a lot of friction. It was also firmly believed that the Japs had informers within the gaol, who received extra rations for their information. There were, however, two radio sets being operated by two Australians. The Japanese were constantly searching for these, so extreme caution had to be taken to see that their operation was strictly limited to a few people. Their location was carefully guarded and constantly changed to escape the snap searches the Japanese carried out. Neither radio was ever discovered.

I spent the first month visiting all those I knew who were still in Changi. However, most of my friends had been sent away on working parties and no news was available on what they were doing. Then one day I received a message to report to Black Jack at his headquarters.

He asked me how I was feeling and told me of the great problem facing the work parties at the airfield construction site. There was a desperate need for a competent interpreter to act as a go-between with the Japanese engineers who were beating up many soldiers each day, mainly because no-one could understand what they were going on about. Black Jack agreed that he had promised me that I wouldn't be included on working parties, but laid it on with a trowel how important it was to try to achieve some harmony with the Japanese on the airfield site. I had no illusions about what I would be in for as I had already heard tales of the brutal treatment that was going on. I also knew that the interpreter often became the new target under these circumstances. Black Jack really hijacked me into the job.

Each morning after a quick meal of rice and soup, hundreds of troops were marched out of the camp with an Australian NCO in charge of groups of about thirty men. On arrival at the airfield, about two miles from the camp, and after much shouting by Japanese or Korean guards, they took over parties of about fifty men. The Japanese engineers roamed around giving orders to the guards. The main task at that time was filling in the swampy ground with soil, brought in by trucks and dumped in heaps. The POWs used either wheelbarrows or baskets to cart the soil to the runway.

One of the tangible benefits of the working parties was that it gave the POWs access to coconuts. Many of the palms had to be cut down and the coconuts were fair game. There were also thousands of Chinese and Malays working on the construction. If the guard was kept occupied, the prisoners could talk to the Chinese and even carry out some trading, swapping items for eggs and any other available food. But every so often someone would be spotted and there would be a howl for the interpreter. I then had to rush to the trouble spot and try to resolve the problem without the guard beating up the soldier ... and maybe me as well.

It was a monotonous job but the Japanese were continually increasing the pressure. They were desperately trying to get the airfield operational. The war was drawing closer and they needed to get their airforce back into Singapore from the islands they were losing. The main war being waged as far as we were concerned was by the doctors in the hospital, trying to keep sick men from being drafted into these working parties. The doctors were magnificent and kept many men out of their clutches by using all sorts of subterfuges. One was to have the Japanese doctor sent in to examine very large numbers, so that it took him all day to see them. Knowing that the Japanese would send another doctor the next day, our doctors would have the new one examine the same men. By doubling the numbers registered as unfit for labour, and by switching some of them with the worst cases on the airfield, our doctors could at least spread the problem over a much larger number.

On the airfield, sabotage was at work as long as the guards and the engineers were not watching. Logs were dumped under the rubble — particularly any logs that would rot quickly. The work went on daily, weekends included, and the airfield slowly took shape. I was becoming increasingly tired but was still able to gather a large number of snails each day to take back to the hospital where they were put to good use.

Changi was a weird community. There was a wide range of clubs, which provided their members with the support so many men desperately needed. Then there were the classes conducted to widen, or provide a basic education. They covered every possible subject and were taken very seriously by both teachers and pupils. Language classes were very popular, but Japanese was not on: no-one was interested knowing how to get into the sort of trouble I was stuck with. Hard as it is to believe, there was actually a yacht club, where sailing was taught to a large number of very interested members. Contract bridge was another of the most popular classes and bridge clubs flourished throughout the officers' lines.

Everything had a value ... things could be swapped ... there was always someone looking for whatever it was you had decided to part with. That is, everyone but me. I had a shirt, a pair of shorts, two pairs of socks and a very good pair of boots that had lain idle for two years. But that was the extent of my possessions. I didn't even have a plate or a mug until the doctors took pity on me and arranged to get me these important items, along with a spoon, knife and fork. Some of the officers still seemed to have a lot of their original gear with them, and even though many of the troops were desperate for clothing, these selfish buggers hung on to their spares with grim determination. The Changi officers' lines contained, I am sad to say, a whole heap of people I had no desire to mix with.

Gossip was on for young and old, and little escaped the eagle eye of some of the worst types. Many enemies were created and some very malicious rumour were spread. Changi was certainly no place to share secrets and I quickly learnt not only to keep my own council but also to avoid a number of officers, many of them high ranking, who handled the truth loosely.

There were also working parties at the wharves and various places in the city, and they had perfected the art of pinching things under the noses of the guards. They were even capable of stealing large items which could be broken apart and carried back into camp by a number of men. For instance, a sewing machine found its way into Changi from one of these working parties, even though all the men were subject to a search at the guardhouse before being admitted back into the camp.

Many of the working parties, especially those working in the city area, were given a number of items to pinch if the opportunity arose. The radios were kept going thanks to items stolen while working in the vicinity of Japanese officers' homes. However, the hardest thing to pinch was food. You were competing with everyone else and the supply available to the local population was at starvation levels. No cats or dogs were ever seen, birds were becoming almost extinct, and every patch of earth that could support a vegetable garden was in use. The Japs could no longer hide the fact that the war was going badly for them. It was obvious to everyone.

I received a message to report to Australian Army Headquarters where, once again, I was put on the spot. The Japanese had called for a new work party of Australians to carry out some excavations in the Kranji area. Captain Stahl was to be in charge of the party, to be known as X3, and I was to be second in charge. The party needed a good interpreter as the work would require explanation. When I mentioned my work at the airfield, the reply was that they would have to do without me. The Kranji job could be dangerous and my superiors thought it was more important that I went there.

Captain Stahl, who was from a Queensland battalion, was a good man and I knew we would get on very well. Doctor Joe Vincent was also to go, and I already had a good rapport with him. A hundred fairly fit men were picked out and, under the supervision of a Japanese sergeant who was to be the camp commander, we were loaded into trucks and transported to a camp near the Kranji Kampong. It was in poor shape, so the sergeant gave us two days to make it habitable. He had twenty Japanese soldiers with him to handle the job and he put them to work too, cleaning up the huts they would occupy. I could see from the start he was a much better type than the average Japanese guard, and he started off by telling me that he would do everything possible to make this a model camp. If the men worked well and behaved, he would make sure that his men treated us accordingly and would also do his best to make available as much food as he could secure. The work was to dig tunnels into a nearby hillside, the story being that they were for ammunition storage. We took this with a grain of salt, as we knew that the Japs were preparing bases from which to fight last-ditch battles, as they had already done in the islands that had been taken from them. At any rate, the sergeant was as good as his word. In fact he was taken to task by his senior officers when they came on inspections because they believed that the POWs could be made to work harder and faster to complete the job.

The work was monotonous rather than hard. At the start, great care was taken to shore up the tunnels. However, as they extended deeper into the hillside it became difficult for those doing the shoring to keep up with the diggers. The ground was very unstable, it was mostly sandy loam, and we had several minor cave-ins. Stahl and I tried to get the two Japanese engineers to slow down tunnelling until the shoring caught up, but they refused. Eventually we had a major cave-in which buried three POWs and a Japanese guard. We managed to dig out the POWs who were still alive, but the guard was dead by the time we reached him. This was a costly lesson, but from then on the tunnels only progressed as fast as the shoring could be carried out.

The war news continued to be bad for the Japanese and we could easily see what was going on. The rations were pitiful, even though the sergeant was doing everything he could to boost them. His men did no better than we did and were continually complaining. The sergeant was having a lot of trouble controlling them and became very morose. I found it increasingly difficult to get through to him.

I had kept a register of each man's weight and condition from the day we arrived. They were losing weight fast and we soon had cases of diphtheria, beri-beri, tropical ulcers and malaria.

Fortunately the sergeant had a good supply of quinine, which he released to us so we were able to control the spread of malaria. Meanwhile the deterioration of the men's health coincided with increased visits from senior Japanese who put the screws on the engineers to increase the work load and working hours. This suggested that the war was quickly moving closer. Even the Japanese guards were put to work to speed up the digging. This caused their tempers to become even shorter and they lashed out at the slightest provocation. Finally the tunnels were finished and we were loaded back onto trucks and returned to Changi.

Our secret radios reported that the Japs were suffering losses in every theatre. Even Tagahashi was said to have asked a group for the latest news from the BBC. All the while those operating the money racket were having a ball. The food position was so critical that those with anything left to sell were prepared to let it go. Suddenly there was a flood of watches and pens. The money was used to buy black-market food of any sort. The price of eggs, peanuts, and fruit and vegetables when they could be bought, skyrocketed. The guards took a hand in this game as they could see the end of the war approaching and were as keen as we were to survive. However, their entry into the black-market increased the price for food.

The camp was alive with rumours. Suddenly all work parties were suspended and we knew the end was close. Then an allied plane dropped leaflets announcing the end of the war. I was told to be available for interpreting work. When a group of paratroopers were dropped on the Changi airfield, on 17 August and their English major was driven to the Area Commander's house, it was final confirmation that the war was over.

SEVENTEEN

The Japanese surrender

On 15 August 1945 the Japanese Emperor spoke over the radio, making the surrender speech. The Japanese people had never before heard his voice over the air.

The previous day, announcements had been made over all stations under Japanese control, telling of the forthcoming broadcast. At the given time Japanese gathered around radio sets across Asia to hear an announcement that left them completely stunned. Most sobbed quietly, but not everyone accepted the speech as freely given.

Few Japanese realised it, but in the days before the surrender, when the Emperor made the surrender tape, a group of young hothead army officers issued false orders to get a number of battalions to surround the Emperor's palace and stop all entry or exit. They firmly believed that the Emperor had been forced to make the speech by the doves in the government and their aim was to prevent the tape being broadcast. A number of senior army commanders were murdered because they would not cooperate. The mutinous officers also took over the radio stations as another means to stop the speech going to air.

The situation continued throughout that day,

but the tapes had been hidden by one of the Emperor's advisers and survived a search. Finally, the commander of one of the battalions checked with a higher ranking officer who told him that he knew of no order to surround the Palace. The battalion commander then confronted the dissident officers, who admitted that the orders had been falsified. They were immediately arrested. The Emperor was furious and insisted that they be punished severely, which they were.

The war was finally over, but there was a state of anxiety in the camp as it was believed that the Japanese were under orders that, in the event of an attack, POWs were to be got rid of first. We also were aware from the news on the camp radio that there was considerable uncertainly that all Japanese commanders would obey the cease fire. This is why the paratroopers were dropped into Changi, to negotiate Admiral Mountbatten's demand for the peaceful handover of Singapore with the Japanese.

Lieutenant Colonel Galleghan and his staff went to General Saito's house to be part of the discussions. I attended, in case additional interpreters were required. Saito was quite arrogant, stating that he had not received official orders from Count Terauchi, the Supreme Commander located in Indo-China. The paratroop major would brook no delay and told Saito that Mountbatten would be landing with his troops within a few days, by which time the Japanese were to have vacated the area around

Changi and started the movement of all Japanese troops onto the Malaysian peninsula. All available food stores were to be made available to the ex-POWs, as well as any medical supplies. The guards were to be disarmed and moved out promptly. Fortunately Lieutenant Tagahashi was able to make Saito realise he could be in serious trouble if he did not obey the Emperor's orders.

Saito capitulated, not too gracefully, but at last he issued the necessary orders and life immediately took on a new dimension for both the ex-POWs and the Japanese on Singapore Island. Camp headquarters immediately took control and mounted our own guards on the gamp area. The Japanese guards were disarmed and our guards used their weapons. Changi overnight became an organised army camp, with strict discipline being enforced.

Within days better rations were available and medical supplies had been dropped by plane. Things looked very different, but everyone was restless awaiting the promised arrival of Mountbatten's troops. In those first few days I took a small party out to see what we could find in some of the large buildings the Japanese had been using. We forced some of the locks and found the buildings crammed with all sorts of items we hadn't seen for years — cases of tinned milk, Marmite, bully beef, cutlery, plates, clothing and, best of all, army boots. We took back as much as we could, intending to return, and were received with open arms.

When I reported what I had found to headquarters, a colonel, whose reputation for being a standover merchant was well known, told me he would charge me if I didn't hand in all we had taken, and that if I went back he would see me in trouble. I felt like swearing at this pompous ass. However, I turned my back on the colonel and walked out. We went back again the next day with a larger number of men and brought back a good quantity of items for those who were short. I had no further contact with the colonel, who I had expected to have a go at me, but he must have thought better of it.

EIGHTEEN

I join the Indian Army

Admiral Mountbatten and his troops landed and soon spread out over the island. Changi became a very busy place as there was so much to be done to get the ex-POWs organised and medically checked before arrangements could be made for their return home. At this time I received a call from our headquarters, where I was stunned to receive an order to report to a Colonel Parkin of the Indian Army. He had requested my services be made available to assist in releasing prisoners from a Sikh POW camp at Kluang on mainland Malaya, just south of Kuala Lumpur, where they had been used as forced labour for airfield construction. The Sikhs were in a pretty desperate situation with up to 90 000 Japanese troops from Singapore and Malaya, many of whom were still armed, being assembled nearby.

I hitched a lift into Singapore and was directed to Indian Army HQ. They had set themselves up comfortably in a civilian house. When I presented my orders to a captain he sent out for some tea and asked me to wait for the colonel. The Indians were very hospitable and I compared this lot with the Sikhs who had treated me so badly when Mac and I had been recaptured.

Colonel Parkin was all you would expect of an Indian Army battalion commander — tall, with a striking personality and appearance. I took a liking to him immediately, though I was a bit stunned when he told me what we were going to do. He and I and two Sikh soldiers were going to drive to Kluang airfield in an open car flying a Union Jack, through the assembled Japanese armies. There we would disarm the Japanese and arrange for a train to being the Sikhs, of whom there were about a thousand, back to Singapore. All we would have was a letter in Japanese from the Japanese Area Commander telling his officers to facilitate our trip and to obey Parkin's orders without question.

All this when we didn't know the state of mind of the Japanese officers in the area we were to go through, or whether the commander of the Kluang POW camp would obey the colonel's orders.

Anyway, Colonel Parkin didn't beat about the bush. I was to be made over into an Indian Army officer and a complete kit was issued to me. It was a great improvement on what I was wearing. At the officers' mess that night I was given a great welcome and we made ready for the trip which was to take place the next day. Somewhere they had got their hands on a very fine Bentley, which looked very grand with its hood down. A Union Jack was mounted on the front right mudguard.

We set out early, knowing we had a lot to do in a short time, and soon crossed over the causeway into Johore Bahru. Once we reached Malaya we were in what was virtually still enemy territory. Every yard of the road had Japanese troops on either side. They were armed and openly displayed their hatred for us, but were not prepared to create any trouble. Some were completely dumbfounded by what they saw. Remember, most of these troops had not received accurate information during the war and had only a distorted idea of who was the victor. Many thought it was only some sort of armistice, so they glared at us as we drove by. Sometimes we were forced to stop by an officer standing in front of us. He usually moved off very quickly when he read the proclamation we were carrying, but troops frequently blocked the road and it took us several hours to complete the drive. Finally we reached the turn-off to the Kluang airfield, and our job was about to begin.

We headed for the gates with a Japanese guardhouse. The guard who came out to greet us was very hostile. He pointed his rifle at us and ordered us to halt. Then the guard sergeant came over to the car with his hand on his sword. They were all very puzzled by our arrival. When I handed him the proclamation, his face was a study, then he went into the guardhouse and rang through to his headquarters. He came back with a completely different look, bowed, returned the document to me and asked that we go through.

We drove slowly into the area, looking at the Sikh ex-POWs. These one proud men, who took pride in their strength, were in terrible condition. They had been brutally treated, and it showed.

As we pulled up in front of Japanese headquarters, two officers met us at the steps. They addressed us in a hostile manner, demanding to know why we were there. I answered them rather roughly, as though I was addressing peasants, which stunned them. Then I gave them the proclamation and they hurried inside the building. I had already advised Colonel Parkin that we would need to put them down quickly and allow no backchat on any matter. He went along with this approach.

A Japanese major then made his appearance. He was obviously the camp commandant and he too started out by being aggressive, but I cut him off at the knees by asking him if he intended to disobey his Emperor's instructions. He went almost white and immediately started to apologise, saying he had no intention of offending us and that he would carry out our orders without question. That was hurdle number one overcome and we could now get down to the real purpose of our visit. Colonel Parkin then stated what he wanted done immediately. It was quite a list of demands.

The Indian leader in the camp was to be called in. The clothing store was to be opened and the Indians given whatever was available. The rations were to be increased immediately. Japanese officers were to hand in all their weapons, including their swords. All Japanese troops except the guards on the gate were to hand in all weapons to the quartermaster's store. Immediate contact was to be made with the railways to have a train ready at nine o'clock the next morning to take all ex-POWs to Singapore. Finally, quarters were to be made available for Colonel Parkin and me for that night, and for the two Sikhs with us.

The Japanese officers were particularly upset at the order to hand in their swords so I had the major's sword placed in the Bentley and locked in the boot so it could not be retrieved. I had already noted two swords that I intended to take back home. They were the captain's and one of the lieutenants, both of which were old family swords.

We left the Japanese to get on with the jobs we had given them and sat talking with the Sikh officer who had been in charge of the POWs. He told us all about the brutal treatment to which he and his men had been subjected, mainly because they refused to join the traitors who had joined Chandra Bose. None of his men had changed sides, even though they would have had a better life. Then he returned to his men to tell them that they would be on a train the next morning for Singapore, and then returned to India.

We spent a peaceful night. Colonel Parkin was happy with the progress we had made and the next morning the Indians, who now looked a good deal better in fresh clothes, marched to Kluang station where the train waited to take them to Singapore. We saw them all under way before we set out back for Singapore, leaving some very disgruntled Japs behind to reflect on their past and to wonder what the future held for them. The Indians would be making reports on war crimes and a few of the Japanese guards would be arrested and tried.

Our trip back was a repeat of the trip up, except that the Japanese on the sides of the road appeared even more aggressive. But although they succeeded in slowing our trip down they didn't cause us any problems we couldn't handle.

Colonel Parkin invited me to stay with his men for a couple of days as it was not known if there were any other Indian POW camps yet to be liberated. I was happy to spend time with these most hospitable people, who were determined to help make up for the past four years.

After two days being spoilt rotten, I made my farewells and was driven back to Changi, which was now a weaving mass of ex-POWs and people from RAPWI — officially Repatriation of All Prisoners of War and Internees, but quickly translated in the camp to mean 'Retain All Prisoners of War Indefinitely', as it was taking so long to get any action. Every day, tempers were becoming more difficult to contain.

Then at long last the exodus began, as vessels became available to start shipping the worst cases out. While I too was keen to get home to see my family, there was the little matter of war crimes that had to be attended to while the events were fresh in our minds. So I spent several days as my time with the Kempi Tai, the Sikhs and in Outram Road gaol were all carefully recorded by legal officers with the incoming forces. By the time I left Singapore many of those I had reported on were in custody and lodged in Outram Road to await trial. I finally arrived home in late September 1945.

The years of imprisonment caused me to reassess my future. I found I was unsure of many things and had great difficulty in handling some of the ordinary day-to-day aspects of civilian life, so Bunny and I decided it might be wise for me to stay in the army for a while until I had a better idea what I would do once I was demobbed. I advised Army Headquarters of this and asked that I be given a posting after the completion of my leave. Within the week I received a letter advising me that I would be required to accept a posting outside the city area. I was to take over as the officer in charge of the Italian POWs based at Wongan Hills.

I accepted, wondering who would be so dopey as to give me such a job.

NINETEEN

Commander of a POW camp

As ordered, I caught the early morning train to Wongan Hills. There were about 150 Italian POWs, all of whom were farmed out to work on properties throughout the district. Wongan Hills was a pleasant country town of about 2000 people north-east of Perth. It had a couple of pubs, a good hospital and a fair range of shops. Most of the nearby properties were well established. I was met at the station by Sergeant Jack Shaw, who was considerably older than me and had probably seen action in the First World War. He spoke fluent Italian, so I was going to need him badly as my skills in that language were exactly nil.

Shaw was a nice friendly guy and I knew at once that he and I were going to get along fine. We drove to what had been a store with offices in front, where I was met by the lieutenant I was to replace. We had a long discussion in what was to be my office, and he gave me a good run-down on each of the POWs and the farmers they were placed with. They were widely spread and I soon realised that it would take a fair amount of time going around checking on them all. The lieutenant told me that he had not had much trouble in the two years he had been there. Some

POWs complained about the farmer and some farmers occasionally had a gripe against the Italians, but such problems were usually solved by moving prisoners from one farm to another.

My command was comprised of Sergeant Shaw, a corporal who acted as orderly room clerk, a driver who was also my batman, a cook and six soldiers. We had a one-cell gaol, in case we had to hold any problematic Italian. My quarters were at one end of the sleeping hut and the sergeant's at the other end, with an eating area and partitioned off soldiers' quarters in between. It was a cosy situation and appeared to be functioning well.

I thought the army had a hole in its head to send me to Wongan Hills, especially to look after POWs, and had not taken into account the fact that I had been away from home for nearly five years. However, I later learnt that they had given me this posting because it was regarded as one of the best in the state. They had not been less than considerate.

For the first few days I got to know the men, checked that our records and correspondence were up to date and met many of the people in the town. They were a nice lot and I thought this would be a fine place to live if you wanted to stay in the country. Once all the checking was complete, I was anxious to get out into the field and meet all those I was responsible for.

Sergeant Shaw and I set out the next morning, taking with us a stock of cigarettes and a range of sweets for any of the POWs who wished to buy them. This was a non-profit operation but made the Italians feel that we were prepared to look after them. Our first stop was the farm most distant from our headquarters, so that we could gradually make our way back and assess what time to return. The farmer was out in the paddock with the Italian, picking rocks and piling them into heaps. I had done this myself when I was young and thought it was a lousy job by anyone's standards. Still, the Italian was happy and greeted the sergeant like an old friend. He spoke quite a bit of English and thanked me for coming to see him. He was very happy, he told me, and he and the farmer seemed to be on good terms so, after spending a reasonable amount of time, we pushed on to the next farm about four miles away.

This was a larger property and there were two Italians working here. Once again, everyone seemed happy. Both of them were smokers and needed cigarettes, as did the farmer, so we sold him some too. The farmer's wife told us that one of the Italians was a fine cook from whom she had learnt a lot, and she would be sad when he had to leave. When she asked me if I had any idea when that was likely to be, I told her I hadn't the faintest idea, but that I'd see what I could find out.

We pushed on to the next port of call, which belonged to an old farmer whose wife had died many years before. He and his Italian worker were like a couple of old cronies. The farmer had learnt a lot of Italian and the POW had made good progress in English. They were very good for each other and I felt that there would be a great problem when the time came for them to part. We stayed and had lunch with them. The Italian was a fine cook and soon had us begging for mercy. I compared this with my time as a POW and told them a little about it. They were both horrified with the idea of rice, nothing but rice.

I could already see what a great success this POW arrangement had been. Everyone was benefiting from it. The POWs were treated with respect, the farmers had never had it so good, and their wives were gaining greater cooking skills. However, Sergeant Shaw said our next call would be different. The farmer was a hard man and the Italian working for him had asked to be moved, but the clash of temperaments was considered a borderline case.

The farmer's wife greeted us and we went into the house to speak with her. When I asked her if the position had improved she said no, so I asked what she thought should be done. She thought for a while and then said that her husband was too hard on the prisoner, whose name was Luigi. But she thought Luigi was also at fault as he got upset very easily. The wife thought it would be fairer to Luigi if we transferred him elsewhere.

This left me with my first decision. Sergeant Shaw and I discussed it at length and we felt a move should be made. I asked if we had any other unhappy Italians and he said there were several who, while not actually complaining, would welcome a change. One of the POWs we would be visiting the next day would probably be better on this property, as he was a very likeable young guy with a very easy nature. I had a chat to the farmer on his own, telling him that I would move his man out in a few days, and he seemed happy. Sergeant Shaw explained the situation to the POW, who was also contented, so we had done the right thing. The two men parted company without animosity. We made one more call that day before setting off back to Wongan Hills.

For the next week we covered a lot of ground and gave a number of POWs advice on a wide variety of subjects. Not surprisingly, most of them wanted to know about their immediate future.

At this stage I had no knowledge of the future situation of the Italian POWs. The sergeant said that my predecessor had often asked Army Headquarters in Perth for clarification but that no decision had as yet been made by Canberra. Apparently it was all bound up with the political position in Italy, so I didn't waste time making any further enquires. As we made further calls on farms, we told the Italians who asked us that we were waiting for the Italian government to sort out the necessary movements.

I quickly discovered that what most of them really wanted was to stay in Australia and bring out their families. You could easily understand this as the letters they received from Italy were not painting a great picture of conditions in their homeland, where there were severe shortages. Australia, on the other hand, offered them many opportunities.

The next month was spent in much the same question and answer situation. I got to know the farms and the POWs better and I received plenty of support from the troops billeted with me. Still, I had to deal with a multitude of individual problems. My days were very full and most satisfying, but I was not happy and felt I had painted myself into a corner. This really wasn't what I wanted for the future. While Bunny was very supportive, she wanted me home with her and the children, full time. On one of my leaves we decided that I would ask for release from the army and we would build a new home. Then I could set myself up in a business of my own.

Once I was satisfied that everything was in perfect order and our work was up to date I wrote to headquarters requesting to be demobbed as soon as they had a replacement for me. After a delay of a few weeks I was notified that my request was agreed to and, as soon as they were able to send a replacement, I was to return to Melbourne and go onto the reserve of officers.

Two weeks later my replacement arrived and I handed my command over to him without delay. The young lieutenant who was to take my place had only been commissioned a year previously, so this represented a great step up for him.

Another week saw me a civilian, after serving over five years in the army. Bunny and I got some plans drawn up for our new house, which was to be built on a fine block she had bought while I was in Changi. It was in Dalkeith, very close to the river. This was to be our dream home, the first we had ever owned. I also saw an opportunity to open a drapery store in Mosman Park, a suburb on the way to Fremantle, so the next six months went swiftly, with a new home coming up and a new business that took off quickly. My business was just what the area needed, turnover started to increase almost from the start, and I soon realised that I could open another shop a few miles away in an area that was being developed. I put on more staff to train and, seeing an opening for frocks, I started a workroom to make our own stock. I found a great lass who had plenty of ideas and talent and she had a well-organised manufacturing operation going in no time, with several girls in training.

By August 1946 we were well settled in our new home and my business was a huge success. Bunny was expecting our third child in December and we felt we had now passed into a new and wonderful world. Our neighbours turned out to be a great bunch and our life was fine in this lucky country, when out of the blue came a message from Army Headquarters in Perth to report to Major Munro. I was informed that I was to be re-enlisted for a short period to go to Tokyo and give evidence at the Major War Trials as one of ten Australian witnesses against the Japanese leaders. I was to be ready to embark on 10 October on the *Kanimbla* in Sydney. I had only a short time to rearrange my business and got my younger brother to act for me while I was away.

TWENTY

Witnesses to war crimes

Australia's ten witnesses to the war trials in Tokyo came from all over the country and were representative of all the areas in which Australians had been brutally treated by the Japanese. Many of us met for the first time when we boarded the *Kanimbla* in Sydney Harbour for our journey to Japan. Also on board were troops for the Occupation Forces, along with stores and supplies, as well as mail. We sailed on 10 October 1946 and called in at Brisbane and Darwin to pick up additional personnel. Each of us was determined to do our best to see that those responsible for the deaths of so many young Australians were made to pay for their crimes. It should be noted that while 4 per cent of POWs in the European theatre of war failed to survive World War II, 35 per cent of those in Japanese hands died.

The trip to Japan gave the ten of us a chance to get to know one another. Each of us was very much an individual, and each of us had remarkable and distressing stories to tell. The other nine witnesses on the *Kanimbla* were:

Brigadier Arthur Seaforth Blackburn, VC: A lawyer and a veteran of World War I and of the Gallipoli landing, Arthur Blackburn was one of only two Australian soldiers to advance far enough to see the shimmering Straits of the Dardanelles before being forced back. It was while serving on the Western Front in July 1916 that Arthur was awarded the Victoria Cross. On return to Australia he resumed his legal career and served for a time as a member of the South Australian parliament.

During World War II, Arthur Blackburn saw action in Syria and his battalion was diverted to Batavia in February 1942 while returning to Australia. As brigadier in charge of Black Force he was captured in March and eventually transferred to Changi. He later headed one of the forces sent to work on the infamous Burma railway, where cruelty and callous disregard for the prisoners' welfare led to thousands of deaths. The highest ranking Australian officer to give evidence at the major war crimes trials in Tokyo, Arthur Blackburn was a gentle, thoughtful man who was all but worshipped by his troops.

Lieutenant Colonel Albert Coates: The Senior Medical Officer for the Australian forces in the Changi POW camp, Coates had served with great distinction in the Malayan Campaign. A medical officer with one of the forces sent to Burma for the construction of the railway, Coates fought with the Japanese continually for better conditions and medical supplies, performed endless surgery under primitive conditions, and coped heroically with POWs suffering from dysentery, beri-beri, malaria, cholera and a host of tropical ulcers and skin disorders. Coates' determination earned him many beatings from his captors, but also their respect, and he saved the lives of countless prisoners under his command. At the war crimes trials he gave evidence of the Japanese High Command's complete lack of any concern for the health of POWs and their deliberate withholding of proper rations and medical supplies.

Captain Vivien Bullwinkel was one of a group of Australian nurses who was evacuated from Singapore just before the surrender. The crowded ship on which she left — a small coastal steamer called the *Vyner Brooke* — was under frequent attack and finally sunk not far from Banka Island, off the coast of Sumatra. Sister Bullwinkel was one of a group of about twenty nurses who swam to shore, only to be driven back into the water and machine-gunned by Japanese soldiers. The sole survivor of the massacre, she was eventually picked up by a Japanese patrol and transferred to a POW camp in Sumatra, where she had to hide her wounds in case it was discovered that she was a survivor of the attack.

Lieutenant Gordon Weynton was a signals officer captured at Singapore in February 1942 and later transferred to Borneo as part of B Force to build an airfield for the Japanese. When an illicit radio was found in the POW camp at Sandakan, after information was given to the Japanese by an informer, one officer was executed and Weynton was sentenced to ten years solitary confinement in Outram Road Gaol. Except for a brief time spent in Changi Hospital he spent the rest of the war in Outram Road and was not released until the Japanese surrender. He gave evidence relating to atrocities he had witnessed at both Sandakan and Outram Road.

Lieutenant Charles van Nooten survived appalling imprisonment conditions on Ambon. After giving evidence relating to these experiences he was seconded to the Second War Crimes Tribunal as an investigating officer, remaining in Japan for a further ten months.

Major Phillip Lyburn Head, who was Legal Officer for 8th Division Headquarters before his capture, was kept busy throughout his incarceration recording all possible information that could be used against his captors.

Private Colin Flemming Brien was one of the recent arrivals in Singapore who was thrown into action with only a few weeks training behind him. He survived many bouts of severe illness and brutal treatment. At one point, the Japanese attempted to behead him, slashed at him with a sword, pushed him into a grave and roughly covered him. He survived to testify against his captors.

Major Kevin Lloyd fought with distinction in the Malayan Campaign and again on Singapore Island, this time with virtually untrained soldiers under his command. As a POW he served with

'A' force on the Burma railway. After giving evidence to the war crimes trials he was seconded to the First War Crimes Commission in Hong Kong, where he served as an investigating officer.

Private Keith Botterill, who was only seventeen when he enlisted, was one of only five POWs to survive one of the most dreadful war crimes ever committed — the death march from Sandakan to Ranau of January 1945 that resulted in the death of over 2500 POWs through starvation, bayoneting or beatings inflicted by sadistic Japanese and Korean guards. The story, which lives in infamy, has been told in detail in a number of histories of atrocities committed against prisoners of the Japanese. At an earlier stage of his captivity Keith Botterill also became one of the few POWs to survive a sentence of forty days confinement in a cage that was exposed to the elements and so small he was unable to stand up. He received no food for seven days, no water for three, and was repeatedly beaten and tortured by the guards.

It is necessary at this stage to say something about the background to the trial of the major war criminals in Tokyo. None us on the *Kanimbla* knew much if anything about the background manipulations at the time, but strong and successful pressure had been brought to bear on the prosecuting nations to see that Emperor Hirohito was not amongst those prosecuted. That pressure came from the United States.

At the war's end most people believed that Hirohito would be charged with being a major war criminal, along with Tojo and the other twenty-seven senior Japanese so charged. And my reading since then had done nothing to convince me that he should not have been. The following brief account of Hirohito's family background and involvement in the conduct of the war seems to make his motives, and his supervisory role in the Japanese war effort, perfectly clear.

Hirohito was born in 1901, at a time of great change in Japan. His grandfather, Emperor Meiji, had taken away the power that the Shoguns had enjoyed for many centuries and took it all into his own hands. He set out to make himself 'The Son of Heaven' with absolute power over all of Japan and it's people. The Constitution drafted into law in 1889 described the Emperor as an 'Absolute Ruler' and this was again made clear in a yearbook of 1944–45, which stated that 'The Emperor cannot be removed from the throne for any reason, and he is not held responsible for any overstepping the limitations of law in the exercise of Sovereignty'. Any such responsibility must be assumed by his ministers of state or other subjects.

Meiji personally controlled the armed forces and supervised attacks on Korea and Taiwan, as well as mainland China, from whom he claimed a large indemnity. Korea and Taiwan became Japanese territory. He was also responsible for the war with Russia, and gave them a good drubbing. By this time the Japanese forces were a power to be reckoned with.

Hirohito grew up under the watchful eye of his grandfather. He was taken from his mother at two and a half months of age and handed over to Count Kawamura, a tough retired admiral. When Kawamura died, Hirohito was moved to a separate cottage near the Palace where he was under the close scrutiny of tutors appointed by his grandfather. When Emperor Meiji died, Hirohito as Crown Prince had to quickly take his place in the affairs of state, the more so as his father was such a poor Emperor.

By the time his father died in December 1926, Hirohito's harsh upbringing had made him a strong, resolute, manipulative ruler — truly 'The Son of Heaven' as created by the Constitution and laws put in place by Emperor Meiji.

Hirohito quickly set out to prepare Japan for the power struggle he knew would be necessary for it to gain dominance in Asia, make room for its expanding population, and secure essential supplies of raw materials needed to fuel Japan's expansion of power. As early as 1933 primary schools in Japan used maps showing Indo China (Vietnam), Siam (Thailand), Straits Settlements (Malaya and Singapore), the Dutch East Indies (Indonesia) and the Philippines, all with the Japanese flag flying over them.

With the defeat of Japan in 1945, public opinion in Australia, New Zealand, The Netherlands, China, England, France and

America was overwhelmingly in favour of trying Hirohito as the major war criminal in the Pacific area. However, President Truman and General McArthur would not agree to any such suggestion as they were determined to use him as a puppet to rule the Japanese nation. Truman, whose only claim to fame was that he agreed to the use of the atom bomb on Japan, was by this time struggling politically and knew that he could improve his standing by reducing the troops necessary to occupy and control Japan.

When Joseph Keenan, the Chief Prosecutor at the trials, left America for Japan he was handed a personal note from Truman which stated that the prosecution should lay off Hirohito, and that there should be no attempt to interrogate any of the Imperial Household. The disreputable Keenan carried out this instruction to the letter. At the same time General McArthur had his expert propaganda team busy creating a new image for Hirohito as an unassuming man whose consuming interest lay in marine biology, and who had no control over events during the war.

I believe that the truth is completely different. Hirohito was an astute and devious manipulator who was way ahead of most of his close advisers, whom he constantly manipulated to achieve his ambitions for Japan's Asian dominance. However, he always ensured that there was a scapegoat to take the blame for every difficult decision if anything went wrong. There are numerous instances of senior officials taking the blame for decisions that are Hirohito's and ritually committing suicide. Hirohito was briefed daily in his War Room at the Palace, those briefings covered every facet of the war, and his personal seal was required on all forces' daily decisions.

Hirohito was instrumental, with his son-in-law, in creating Unit 731. An experimental unit set up in Manchuria under the notorious General Shiro Iishi, Unit 731 employed hundreds of scientists seeking to develop new forms of biological warfare. At least 12 000 lives were sacrificed to their experiments. The victims included English, Chinese, Australian and Russians, all of whom were murdered once they had outlived their usefulness. General Iishi hid after the war, but a deal was made by General Macarthur's Headquarters and he was granted immunity from prosecution in exchange for passing on the results of his research.

Hirohito ordered the execution of all the airmen captured after the Doolittle raid on Tokyo.

He arranged for the printing of 'occupation money' for all the countries Japan overran, money which was printed in September 1940, well before the war commenced.

He gave his approval for the construction of the Thai–Burma railway and for the use of POW and native labour.

In 1943 his close friend and adviser Kido raised with Hirohito the very gruesome details of the Bataan death march. Hirohito refused to discuss it.

The list is selective, but horrifying. Yet after

the war Hirohito discarded and distanced himself from all his previous close associates, amongst them Marquis Koichi Kido, Prince Fuminaro Konoye, Lieutenant General Hideki Tojo and Prince Saionji, all of whom had served him with absolute loyalty. He distanced himself from them immediately, to try to give the impression that he was not party to their decision.

There is ample evidence that Hirohito was responsible for many of the war crimes his forces committed, both directly and indirectly. By pursuing the myth of his divinity and stressing the disgrace of becoming a prisoner he not only brought about the needless death of many thousands of his own troops, but also helped foster the low regard his armed forces showed Allied POWs. If any further proof is required, then remember where Australians now lie buried — in Java, Borneo, Ambon, Timor, New Guinea, the Solomons, Sumatra, Malaya, Singapore, Burma, Japan, Vietnam, China, Manchuria and Thailand. A number of them died in battle, but the bulk of them died of starvation, lack of medical treatment, torture and brutal beatings.

And as the war drew closer to Japan and nearer its end, the Japanese leaders, whose orders were all approved by Hirohito, ordered that the retreating Japanese forces kill all POWs, who had already endured up to three and a half years of inhumane treatment. A copy of that order survived the war and was presented to the Tokyo War Crimes trial.

Outside Hitler, no leader has ever been responsible for so much misery and death in his lifetime. In my opinion, and that of countless others, Hirohito was a major war criminal.

Nonetheless, the months immediately after the war saw a war of words as those who wanted to use the Emperor to their own advantage fought to have him excluded from prosecution or even close scrutiny. Over the ensuing years secret documents have been released that show the degree of agitation this decision caused amongst the Allies.

TWENTY-ONE

Japan

On the trip to Tokyo, Brigadier Blackburn and I seemed to have an immediate rapport and we spent much of our time walking around the decks talking. He was a quiet, gentle man with a great sense of humour and not much time for the social scene. He also had a fund of knowledge and an inquiring mind and we decided that, when we reached Japan, we would use any spare time to see what we could of the country.

The voyage passed quickly and we arrived in Yokohama on 30 October, where we were met by members of the Tokyo War Crimes Commission and taken to our accommodation at Empire House in the Marunouchi district of Tokyo. This had been the main business district before the war and was only a short distance from the Emperor's Palace. Empire House was well set up, with separate rooms for each of us, a small but efficient canteen, and a separate desk clerk for each floor, who held your key when you were out. Security was very tight and we had no problems during our stay.

Mr Justice Mansfield, the Chief Australian prosecutor, was in charge of our party. He told us it would be a while before we would be called and that we could use our time until then as we wished. He did, however, suggest that we all spend a few days in the Tribunal, to see how it functioned. Beyond that, all he asked was that we advised his office where we could be located if we intended staying out of the building overnight. We were all issued with passes to the Tribunal so we could observe the procedure.

Arthur Blackburn and I decided to stay together and agreed it made sense to spend a few days in the courtroom before we made any attempt to explore Tokyo and nearby Japan.

The courtroom was in itself quite a set-up — just like an American film stage. On one side was a raised bench behind which sat the eleven judges, one from each of the Allied countries mounting the prosecution. Along another wall in two tiers sat the defendants, with a number of military police behind them. On the opposite wall was a glassed-in area with interpreters from each of the countries represented. There was considerable space given over to the large numbers of lawyers for the defence and the prosecution. As well, there was a limited area set aside for observers and the general public.

The procedure was that the prosecutor from the same country as the witness would ask questions in the witness's native tongue. Questions and answers were translated into the various languages and then passed through headphones to the defendants and all other members taking part in the proceedings. As you can imagine, it was a slow and boring procedure. Arthur Blackburn and I spent three days listening to evidence being given by Filipino witnesses. As it seemed they would be giving evidence for at least another week we decided to explore those parts of Japan we could reach easily.

I had already done a bit of research with some of the Japanese running Empire House and had a list of places we could visit and a number of hotels, including several inns (ryokans) where gaijins (foreigners) did not usually stay because of language problems. Arthur and I planned to spend three days in the Nikko area, where 15 000 artists and artisans had been brought from all over Japan in the seventeenth century to build the shrine for Tokugawa Ieyasu, Japan's most powerful Shogun who unified the country which enjoyed peace for the next 250 years. The shrine and mausoleum took twenty years to complete and are set in a 200 000 acre national park. The shrine features a number of buildings distinguished by their intricate carvings and panelling. The Shoguns and their emissaries also had a lovely vermilion painted bridge to cross the swiftly flowing Daiyagawa River. For three centuries, this bridge could not be crossed by any other persons. The whole area is surrounded by 300-year-old cedar trees. It is a place of great beauty and steeped in Japanese history and culture.

We knew these side trips may be difficult in some ways, as we were not certain whether the shrines were open or the hotels were back in business, but I was certain that I could handle any problem we came up against. The currency was also in a mess and the main things that had value wherever you went were cartons of American or English cigarettes and tins of meat, so we made sure that we got plenty of both from the canteen to take with us, as well as sweets for the children. Arthur wore his uniform with the red tabs on his shoulders and the red band on his cap and the Japanese immediately moved to assist him in out of deference to his rank. I was just regarded as his aide.

One service that had been maintained and was operating smoothly was the railways. Japan did not at this time have a well-developed system of roads and road transport but the rail system had been continually upgraded to provide an efficient service to all parts of the country.

We left from the Tokyo main station by what was called a limited express, which took us two and a half hours to reach Nikko. We passed through great devastation in the Tokyo area but once we moved into the country everything appeared normal. The farmers were working in their fields and the villages looked as though nothing had happened. When we arrived at the Nikko station the people were poorly dressed but did not seem to be affected in any other way by the war. We had hoped to talk with some of them on the journey, but the stationmaster made sure that we had a compartment to ourselves and there was no way he would allow anyone else to enter.

Not that I think too many Japanese would have wanted to be in the same compartment as a high ranking officer: they would be too uncomfortable.

At any rate, we started to make our first contacts with the Japanese people on the station at Nikko. Several of them were helpful and one fetched us an old taxi to take us to the Nikko Kanaya Hotel. The proprietors were very proud of the fact that Charles Lindberg, Eleanor Roosevelt, David Rockefeller and many other Western celebrities had stayed with them pre war. Now they had us in their visitors' book and they gave us a beautiful old room with a view over the river to the Sacred Red Bridge. Not many gaijin had stayed overnight in Nikko and we were given the royal treatment. Arthur loved every minute of our stay.

The local shops were small but to our surprise were well stocked with wonderful lacquer ware and we were able to get some examples of these lovely pieces for a very nominal cost. I was only sorry that some of the pieces that we both loved were too big and awkward for us to cope with.

When I enquired whether the shrine was open I discovered that it was. In fact it had never been closed during the war. Apparently many Japanese visited it and the nearby Lake Chuzenji to escape from the worry of the conflict. We walked to the shrine and spent some time admiring the very beautiful Sacred Bridge which the Japanese know as Shinkyo. There was an entry fee to the shrine but the attendants took one look at Arthur and waved us through, bowing until we had passed. There were a number of Japanese also visiting, so we were able to ask them any questions that we had. Their answers, however, were not as simple as our questions and often difficult to follow.

However, the buildings were full of interesting items and intricate carvings and we spent many hours in the Rinnoji Temple, the Sanbutsudo Hall with its three wooden images of the Buddha plated with gold leaf, and the Toshogu Shrine which contains the Shogun's tomb. It is stated that 2.4 million sheets of gold leaf were used in the buildings. Up further flights of stairs is the Yomeimon Gate, also known as the twilight gate as it is said it takes from daylight to twilight to see everything carved onto it. And above the gate to the royal stables are three carved monkeys — the original carving of the 'See no evil, hear no evil, speak no evil' famous around the world.

Arthur and I spent many happy hours exploring this wonderfully preserved part of Japanese history. Lake Chuzenji, about an hour's bus ride up a winding mountain road, was also beautiful and peaceful and we were quiet and contented when we got back to our hotel for a splendid evening meal, followed by a hot bath. During the night we both awoke to feel the building moving. It was our first experience of an earth tremor, of which there are many hundreds a year in Japan.

Our journey back to Tokyo was much like our

trip up. The stationmaster made sure that we had a compartment to ourselves, in fact he made two young men get out and go into another, and wouldn't hear of them joining us. We rewarded him for his attention with a couple of packets of cigarettes which he could flog on the black market probably for the equivalent of his week's pay. On this and later trips we gave packets of cigarettes to anyone we felt had been of service to us knowing that they would rather have them than Japanese money.

Nothing had changed back at Empire House, other than we both received an invitation from one of the British battalions to a dance they were holding. Social events in Tokyo were very much American-run and controlled and other nationalities did not get invitations. You could have been on another planet and if there is anything that sticks in my memory about my time in Japan, it is that the Americans as a group are bad news. Individually, they are fine, but as a mass they are not my cup of tea.

I checked with Judge Mansfield's office, where I was assured that there was no way we would be needed for some time yet, so Arthur and I went into a huddle and decided our next trip should be to Hakone and Mount Fuji. Once again with our supply of cigarettes and bully beef, we fronted up to the Tokyo railway station. I bought two tickets to Odawara, and with the usual performance the stationmaster made sure we had a compartment to ourselves. For the twenty miles or so from Tokyo to Yokohama the whole distance was just a mass of burnt-out buildings as far as the eye could see. This was the result of the American fire bombing near the end of the war and all that remained of the wooden buildings were their tall chimneys.

Odawara was a small town where we changed to a two-carriage narrow-gauge hill train which wound its way up through the mountains. The carriages were crowded and this time we were able to join the locals — as well as their livestock. Several had chooks, two had small pigs, and many had bundles of vegetables. Everyone was cooperative and happy to share their trip with a couple of gaijin. They were all curious to know where we were going, and when they found out they started to tell us all about their trips up Mount Fuji. If one could believe them, most had made the trip to the top. When I assured them that we only intended to view Mount Fuji from afar they told us about Lake Ashi, or Lake Hakone as foreigners know it, and where we could stay. The trip was fascinating and full of good humour. These people were farmers who knew little of war, and to them there were many other things that were more important.

After a night at the beautiful Fujiya Hotel in Miyonoshita we picked up the small train once more and travelled with another group of interesting country folk to Hakone, where we got off to spend some time at the lake with its magnificent view of Mount Fuji. We were taken to the Ryokan Ichinoyu by an old man with his small horse and cart. The ryokan was at least 350 years old and generations of the one family had operated it continuously.

For the first time in our travels we had a typical Japanese ryokan room with tatami matting. We removed our shoes at the entrance and moved around in slippers. Our room had a low lacquer table with a pit beneath it which housed a habachi — a large porcelain tub filled with burning charcoal which was the mainstay of Japanese heating. All bedding was hidden in cupboards behind sliding doors and only brought out when needed. The toilets were communal, men and women using the same ones, but no-one except us seemed to notice. An alcove had a large wooden tub and our servants wanted to know when we would like our bath. If required, our back would be scrubbed for us. Arthur seemed a little diffident but I assured him that this was the custom, no one took the slightest notice of another body, so he too enjoyed the fine service available.

This was a great introduction to old Japan and we enjoyed it thoroughly, but our meals, which were served in our room by two maids, were another matter. There were only Japanese style dishes and I tried to organise food that would be most acceptable to our tastes. But while our meal was pleasing to the eye, it was not to the palate. Raw fish was a new experience, most of the vegetables were ones we had not seen before, and the green Japanese tea was too bitter for our tastes. Our beds were also a new experience. The futons were extremely comfortable but the pillows were far too hard for us, so I asked if there was anything soft we could use. The staff were mortified that they had not realised that gaijin do not use hard pillows and brought us some soft cushions with white covers. The maids and the manager bowed and apologised so profusely it was as if an international incident had taken place.

Next morning we had what was apparently a traditional Samurai breakfast. The tray, as usual, was beautifully presented, with a flower in a stemmed vase, beautiful crockery and plenty of rice steaming in a wooden tub. There were dishes of strange vegetables, lots of tofu, and what appeared to be squid. We made a reasonable meal, mostly of rice with occasional pieces from the other dishes. The plums turned out to be extremely salty, so they got a miss, but it had been a fascinating experience and the charge was reasonable, so we had nothing to complain about. The old man and his cart was recalled and took us to the edge of the lake, which gave us a splendid view of Mount Fuji.

We caught our little train back to Odawara, where we picked up the train back to Tokyo. Once again the stationmaster emptied out a compartment for us in what was a full train. I think the railway staff must have had instructions to not take any chances if they thought an officer was high ranking, and to make sure he got the full treatment. Arthur and I didn't mind at all.

Apart from anything else it meant we could sleep if we wanted to.

Back in Tokyo there had been no real progress. The Filipinos were only getting towards the end of their evidence, and then I believe the Dutch would start. The weeks were flying by and I was starting to worry. We had not received any mail since leaving Australia. I had written many letters to Bunny and I am sure she had written regularly to me, but nothing was getting through. It was now well into November and Bunny was due to give birth to our third child in the last week of December. I had only agreed to come to Japan on the assurance that I would be back with my wife before the birth. No-one seemed to be able to say why none of us were receiving mail, other than to say that communications between Japan and Australia were not very satisfactory. This seemed a gross understatement. Judge Mansfield sent a cable to find out what was happening, and to see that Bunny was informed of the mail delays. Two days later we received an apology. The mail had been sidetracked and would soon arrive but Bunny was well and everything was going normally.

Around this time I had cause to visit the Dai Ichi Building which was General McArthur's Headquarters. Naturally it was the most impressive building at that time in Tokyo and faced the plaza in front of the Emperor's Palace. I went into the foyer and headed for the lifts, but as I entering one I was picked up bodily by two massive Negro MPs who took me out, walked me over to the foyer and told me to keep out of the lifts, which were for General McArthur's exclusive use. 'Go up the stairs,' one of them said, as rude as you like. It was about the same standard that I found in any dealings with the Americans in Tokyo. We were the pits in their eyes, just a bit lower than the Dutch or Filipinos. I made no further attempt to make contact with any Americans, and returned to the Tribunal that afternoon to see what progress was being made. What I saw and heard did nothing to change my attitude towards Americans.

It was more like a circus than a trial. Joseph B. Keenan, the American prosecutor, had the floor and I am certain he was as full as a bull. His words were slurred and I had great difficulty in following him. The Chairman, Sir William Flood from Australia, was furious and kept making Keenan repeat what he said. Even then I don't think he knew what Keenan was on about. The defendants and their lawyers were all nearly asleep and Keenan was making a farce of the whole process.

I watched the face of Tojo as he sat with the other defendants, trying I think to get some understanding of what Keenan was talking about, but he finally took off his earphones so I presume he too had had enough. Not that the Japanese cared a tinker's what went on in here. They had closed their minds to the whole event and they would never accept any punishment that this court dished out as fair. The defendants were already heroes and nothing would change that. Their names would appear on the rolls in the Shrine for Heroes, along with others in their history. In the opinion of most Japanese, the trial was for the benefit of the relatives of the soldiers who fought and died on the Allied side and the Japanese were simply following the advice that their Emperor gave them in his surrender speech to the nation — to 'bear the unbearable, and to endure the unendurable'. Just about every Japanese knew Japan would rise again and one day lead Asia.

When you looked at these two rows of old feeble men in the defendants' box it was hard to believe that they caused so much pain and anguish to so many people. They looked nondescript and you could pass any of them in a crowd without noticing them, yet fate had thrown them into positions of extraordinary power and they had wilfully exploited this power to feed the vanity of the self-styled 'Son of Heaven' who, like Pontius Pilate, was denying their existence to save his own skin.

Every day that I attended this trial made me firmer in my belief that the wrong people were on trial and that by letting the real culprit escape justice, we were giving the wrong signals to the rest of Asia. During my stay in Japan I had a number of discussions with a variety of men of different ages, and one thing they had in common was a clearly defined belief in the Japanese nation.

Hidden just below the surface was an equally clear sense that the Japanese were the real leaders of Asia and would take their place again one way or another. Time has shown just how accurate this belief was.

Meanwhile, Arthur was keen to see a kabuki play so I made enquiries again from my buddies down at the front desk. They immediately got us tickets for a show that night at the kabuki theatre near the Ginza, Tokyo's main thoroughfare. Neither of us had much of an idea what we were in for, but we knew all parts in kabuki are played by men and it is a very much sought after position to play the female roles. The plays are all about the past, the Japanese love and adore them, and they are often so long that one starting at 10 a.m. might not finish until 5 p.m.

We had good seats and waited expectantly for the curtain to rise. We had been given a sheet with a synopsis printed in very quaint English, so at least we knew what the play was going to be about, but I didn't know if I would be able to follow the Japanese as much of it would be in old dialects. The play told the story of a Samurai who became a drunk and in so doing put his master's life in danger. After facing many perils his master was wounded because of the Samurai's carelessness, so he had to finally take his life. It was all very dramatic and much of the action took place in a geisha house where the master had a favourite geisha whom he supported.

The play was really brilliant and Arthur

enjoyed every minute of it. My translations were pretty sketchy but they conveyed the main themes and events. Afterwards we decided to walk back to Empire House. It was a fine night but getting very cold and you could see the Japanese did not have enough heavy clothing. Most of what they wore was synthetic and would not keep out the cold of the approaching winter. We could see their envious looks at our thick warm army overcoats and I am sure most of them would have traded pretty well anything they owned to secure such a garment.

We still had plenty of time to make another trip so we left our itinerary with Justice Mansfield's office and again prepared to take off, this time for three nights on the Izu Peninsula, which was famous for a number of reasons. It is where Admiral Perry anchored his ships on his first trip to Japan, where Harris Townsend set up his American Embassy when he was allowed to do so, and where he lived with his mistress Tojin Okichi, who drowned herself when Townsend left and she was ostracised by the Japanese. The Izu Peninsula is also a great holiday area with its large number of hot mineral spa areas.

Our trip was an enjoyable one, but when we returned we found that everyone at Empire House was getting edgy. Not being able to speak Japanese, most of them lacked the confidence to venture far, and what little post-war Tokyo offered they had already seen. At long last some mail arrived. I received ten letters from Bunny, and caught up with what had been happening in Dalkeith. My young brother who was standing in for me at my business had pranged my car, but it was being repaired. More importantly, Bunny was getting anxious that I mightn't be home, as promised, for the birth of our third child. I sat down and wrote her a long letter, telling her what was going on in Tokyo and renewing my promise to be home in time, no matter what.

Arthur's wife was also getting restless about how long he was likely to be away and I think we were all becoming tired of the dreary, and in many ways, unsatisfactory way the trial was progressing. Most of us already regretted that we had agreed to come.

I went and had an interview with Justice Mansfield, with whom I had a good relationship. It was already December and I wanted to make it clear to him exactly where I stood. He knew about my agreement with the army and assured me that if we didn't get a clear picture soon he would release me to return home and I would have to give my evidence through a sworn affidavit. We set a date of 15 December for me to complete my evidence and he would try and get the court to agree to take me out of sequence. From now on Arthur and I had to stay in Tokyo but we still managed to visit some interesting places, including Ueno Park, where the National Museum is located.

Two days were spent completing a sworn affidavit with Justice Mansfield's legal officer, in case I was denied the opportunity to give my evidence in person. As yet no decision had been made by the office of the Chief Prosecutor, but I didn't hold out much hope that the drunk Keenan would agree. Time proved me right, and when I went to see Judge Mansfield, he told me that the Chief Prosecutor's office had turned down my request to have my evidence heard out of sequence. None of the Australians would be giving the Tribunal any evidence until well into the New Year.

True to his promise, Mansfield released me immediately. I was free to make whatever arrangements I could to get home and he would advise Australia accordingly.

TWENTY-TWO

Homeward bound

Now I was free to find my way home, but there was no help for me from official sources, as there were no organised trips on a regular basis between Japan and Australia. There was, however, an RAAF unit at the airport, so I got a taxi and headed out there. This unit was only very small, its main job being to service and handle any incoming traffic — mostly VIPs, cargo and mail. One of the ground staff directed me to the office of Flight Lieutenant Brad Rodgers, who was in charge of the unit.

Brad was about my own age and he heard me out as I explained my situation. When I told him of my promise to be home in time for my third child's birth he said he knew just how desperate I must be. He had been unable to be with his wife for their second child as he had been posted to Tokyo. All the air force had moving was a mail plane with some cargo which was due to depart the next day. Officially they were not allowed to carry any passengers, but if there was room on the plane and the captain agreed, Brad would let me go.

I was ecstatic. I had imagined great difficulty in getting the unit commander to let me on a plane and considered myself very lucky that he understood my predicament so well. However, I still had to hurdle of getting the captain to agree. After all, he was the one taking the big risk, as the real problem would develop when we landed at an air force base in Australia. I headed back to pack and say farewell to the rest of the gang, especially Arthur Blackburn who had proved such a good friend. I thanked the staff on the front desk at Empire House who had been so helpful, had a good meal and a hot bath, then went early to bed. My trip back, if it happened, would not be a bed of roses on a cargo plane.

Breakfast over, I made my last goodbyes and headed once again for the airport. The plane had not yet arrived as it had run into a headwind. When it finally landed, there was nothing glamorous about this old DC3, which looked as though it had been working hard for a long time. The captain came into the office and Brad Rodgers introduced me to Flight Lieutenant Colin Smith. Fortunately he was another youngish man who immediately say yes; I could go with them as far as the Batchelor base in the Northern Territory, but I would have to hop out under instructions when they could smuggle me off the base. The authorities, he said, were paranoid about anyone carrying unauthorised passengers, but he seemed to welcome the attack on rules he didn't agree with.

The plane had a lot of cargo to unload and needed service to both engines, so Smith decided that we should not take off until the following morning to allow the ground staff time enough to spend on the service. I spent the night with the crew in their quarters at the drome. They were interested to hear about the Tribunal, which they thought was a waste of time unless all the war criminals were executed to make up for what had happened.

Next morning we said goodbye to Brad Rodgers and took off. There were four of us on the plane — the captain, the navigator, a wireless operator and myself. There wasn't much cargo, but it included a lot of mail and personal gear for some troops who had returned previously. The crew had seats and some comforts but I had to make myself as comfortable as I could in the body of the plane. The vibration was pretty bad and it was very noisy, but the throbbing of the engines soon made me drowsy and I fell asleep for a while. We were heading for Samah in the Philippines, where we would refuel for the next leg.

At about midday the wireless operator woke me and said we were about an hour out of Samah but were having trouble with one engine. We would have to dump everything we could to lighten the plane as it didn't fly too well on one engine and they would soon have to feather the troublesome one. I was to help him dump all we could get rid of. The wireless operator opened the back door and I shoved things down to him — bags of mail, trunks, parcels. Whatever was loose, it all went. Finally he shut the door and told the captain it was all gone. No wonder the mail was so unreliable!

We were slowly losing height and weren't sure that we could make it to Samah, but finally the field came in view and we were allowed to come straight in to land. We had just made it with little to spare. When we taxied up to a hangar and got out I felt like kissing the ground.

Just a short distance away there was another grounded plane from Australia. We were told it had been carrying the Papal Nuncio, and it too had developed engine trouble and had to land on one engine. Perhaps God, having let the Papal Nuncio land, had to balance the budget by approving our landing also. At any rate, we now had to face a stop-over on Samah until the repairs could be carried out. It would be at least twenty-four hours before we could hope to get away. There were several rooms we could use at the drome, but we would have to get meals at a nearby village. Fortunately I still had a few cartons of Players cigarettes so we had the currency to ensure that we ate well. And so we did. I even bought some wooden carved clogs, also purchased with cigarettes, to take home to Bunny.

When the work was completed on the plane, the captain was particularly careful to make sure that it had been carried out to his satisfaction. We were refuelled and took on food and coffee for the next leg to Lae, from where we would make the final run to Batchelor air base, outside Darwin. The trip was without any further incidents and when we landed at Batchelor we taxied to a position close to the perimeter wire. The crew got out, and I waited. After a short time the captain returned to say that they were to proceed to Adelaide after refuelling and I could go with them, In the meantime I had to keep out of sight and not speak while the ground staff were refuelling the plane.

Soon we were on our way again. It was great to be back in Australia and every hour was getting me closer to home. The trip to Adelaide was uneventful, although my heart was in my mouth when we hit a number of air pockets and dropped sharply a few hundred feet. Still, we landed in Adelaide without incident and it was easy for me to sneak away from the plane after saying goodbye to these great guys who had saved my bacon. I will always remember them for the help they gave a stranger. Risking trouble, and without even a hint of gain, was an example of genuine Australian mateship.

Now I was at the last hurdle. There were only two ways home, but the train was too slow and the army was usually reluctant to approve plane transportation. With nothing to lose, I headed for the railway station and the Transit Officer's office. When I explained my problem he was completely unsympathetic. He wouldn't have a bar of me or my story. All he wanted was authorisation for my trip, but I had none other than Justice Mansfield's letter releasing me from the war crimes trials. I could see that this army type was incapable of doing anything on his own, so I got mad with him and gave him a choice. Either he gave me a pass to travel by plane to Perth or I would go to the Adelaide papers and tell them how he had refused to give me a pass to get home to my wife in time for the birth.

I must have struck a chord of humanity, or more likely of fear, but suddenly he gave me a pass to get a ticket on a commercial flight to Perth. Within hours I was on the last lap of my trip home. I slept most of the way, as the last few days had been without much sleep. At Maylands airport I got a taxi and headed for Minora Road and my family. You can imagine my wife's face when I came through the back door, and the two kids gave me a hero's welcome.

Two days after I got home the phone rang. It was army headquarters ringing to advise Bunny that they had contact with Tokyo and all was well and they would let her know when I was coming home. 'Well, that's great,' she said, 'but you're a little late. He's already here. Would you like to speak to him?' There was a deathly silence and then finally the officer said, 'Well, tell him to come in and see us next week.' I did just that, and so ended my trip to Japan. I had come home without the army's help and the total cost was a few packets of cigarettes and a plane fare from Adelaide.

I was back in the lucky country, and could get on with my life.

APPENDIX

The Tokyo War Crimes Trial

The International Military Tribunal Far East commenced in January 1946 and all Allied countries were asked to submit lists of major war criminals. The final lists were agreed to by representatives of the Allied nations — twenty-eight warrants were issued and those arrested were lodged in Sugamo Prison.

Prince Konoye committed suicide the night before his arrest and two others on the final list — Matsuoka, a former Foreign Minister, and Nagano head of the Naval Staff — both died before the trials started, leaving the following to face the Tribunal:

Age	Name	Previous position	Sentence
64	Tojo Hideki	Premier	Hanging
63	Itagi Seishiro	Minister of War	"
70	Matsui	Commander, China	"
56	Muto	Chief of Staff	"
70	Hirota	Premier & Foreign Minister	"
65	Doihara Kenji	Commander, Foreign Troops	"
60	Kimura	Vice-Minister of War	"

Age	Name	Previous position	Sentence
66	Umezu Ushijiro	Chief of Staff	Imprisonment
61	Shimada Shigetaro	Navy Minister	"
66	Togo Shinori	Foreign Minister	"
59	Kido Koichi	Keeper of Privy Seal	"
69	Hata Shunroku	War Minister	"
81	Hiranuma Kuchiro	Premier, 1939	"
56	Hoshino	Manchuko Official	"
56	Hashimoto	Colonel	"
59	Kaya	Finance Minister	"
68	Koiso	Premier, 1944	"
77	Minami Jiro	War Minister	"
58	Oka	Chief of Naval Staff	"
62	Oshima	Ambassador to Germany	"
62	Sato Kenryo	Chief of Military Affairs	"
61	Shigatori	Ambassador to Italy	"
60	Shigamatsu	Ambassador & Foreign Minister	"
60	Suzuki Teichi	Chief of Planning Board	"
71	Araki	Foreign Minister	"

All those not hanged were given long prison terms,

with the exception of Shigamatsu, who received only seven years.

All those tried as major war criminals were known as A Grade prisoners; a further twenty field commanders were classed as B Grade prisoners; and the number of C Grade prisoners ran into thousands. B and C Grade prisoners were tried in tribunals held in Singapore, Manila, Shanghai, Guam, Jakarta and several other centres.

The American-held courts tried 1200 persons, of whom 222 were executed, 153 were acquitted, and 825 were imprisoned.

British, French, Chinese, Dutch, Philippine, Australian and New Zealand courts tried 3200 prisoners, of whom 732 were executed, 396 were acquitted, and 2072 were imprisoned.

No figures are available of those tried by Soviet courts.

As for my torturers, Lieutenant Tanashi and Sergeant Amura, I understand that they were posted to Burma when the going got tough and did not return.

The Major War Tribunal in Tokyo was convened in April 1946 and continued through until April 1948, during which time 419 witnesses gave their evidence in person, 779 gave theirs by affidavit, and 4336 exhibits were admitted as evidence. The prosecution was estimated to cost in excess of $US6 million.

After the trials finished it took six months for the verdicts to be completed. The findings were delivered to the court by the Chairman of the Tribunal, Sir William Webb, an Australian who had already acted as President of the War Tribunal Trials in Manila and who had stated his belief that Hirohito deserved to stand trial as a Major War Criminal.

The sentences were given for each defendant on 12 November 1948.

General McArthur then assembled the representatives of the eleven prosecuting powers to hear their views on the sentences, before making his final judgment.

America, China, New Zealand, the Philippines, Britain and the USSR all voted that the sentences stand as given.

France voted for no change, but for clemency to be applied.

Australia voted for no change, but would not oppose reduced sentences.

Canada was not opposed to a reduction in sentences.

India voted that all death sentences be commuted to life imprisonment.

Holland voted for mitigation of five of the death sentences.

On 24 November McArthur confirmed the sentences without alteration and ordered that the death sentences be carried out a week after 25 November. However, the executions were delayed by an appeal lodged at the United States Supreme Court, which was promptly rejected, and the sentences were carried out on 23 December 1948.

The bodies of the seven war criminals were cremated and the ashes scattered to ensure that there could be no later canonisation by the Japanese.